Colour YOUR OWN MANGA

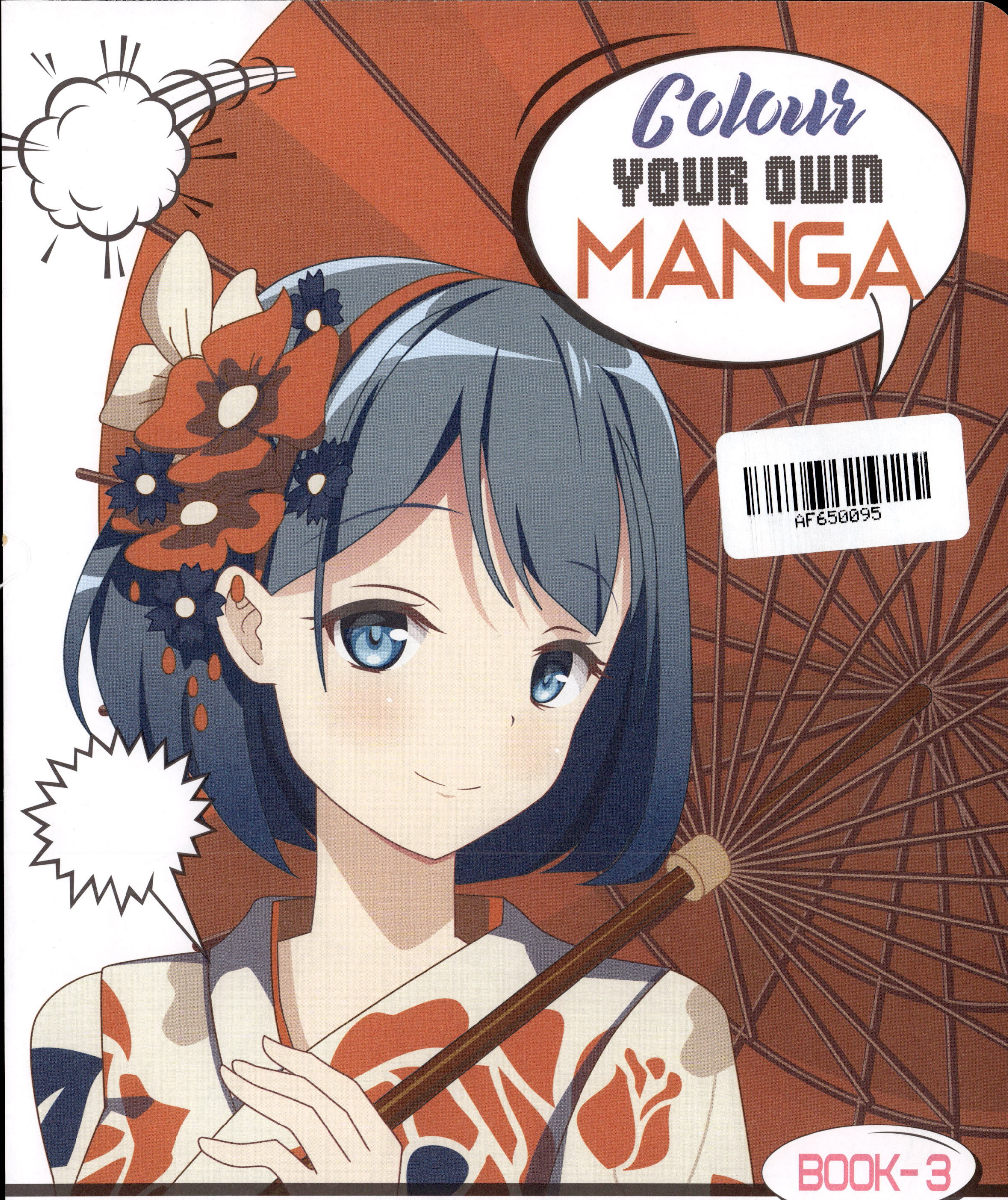

BOOK-3

DREAMLAND PUBLICATIONS

J-128, Kirti Nagar, New Delhi-110 015, India
Tel.: +91-11-2510 6050, 2543 5657 • E-mail : dreamland@dreamlandpublications.com
Shop online at www.dreamlandpublications.com
Follow us on www.instagram.com/dreamland.publications

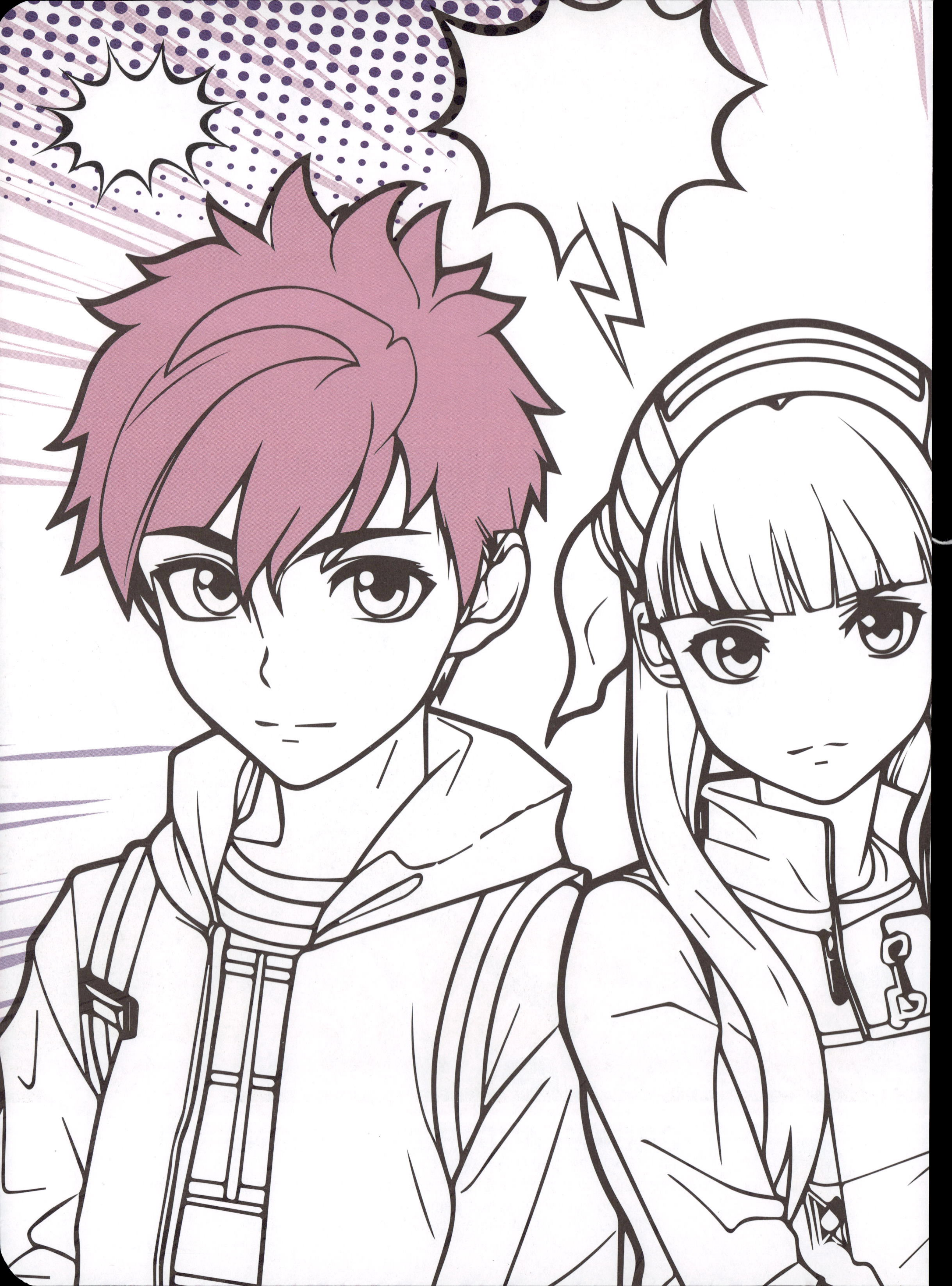

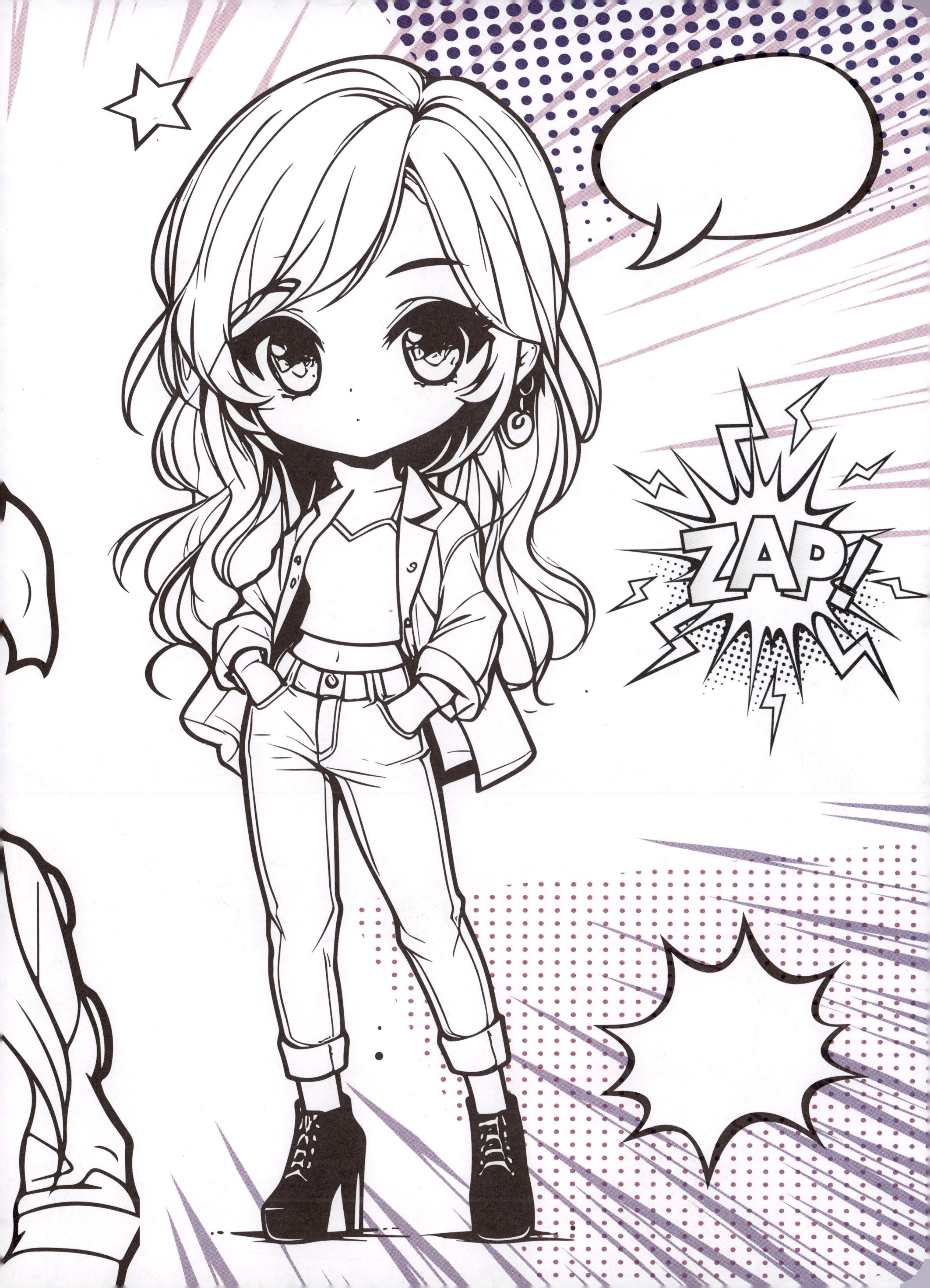
ZAP!

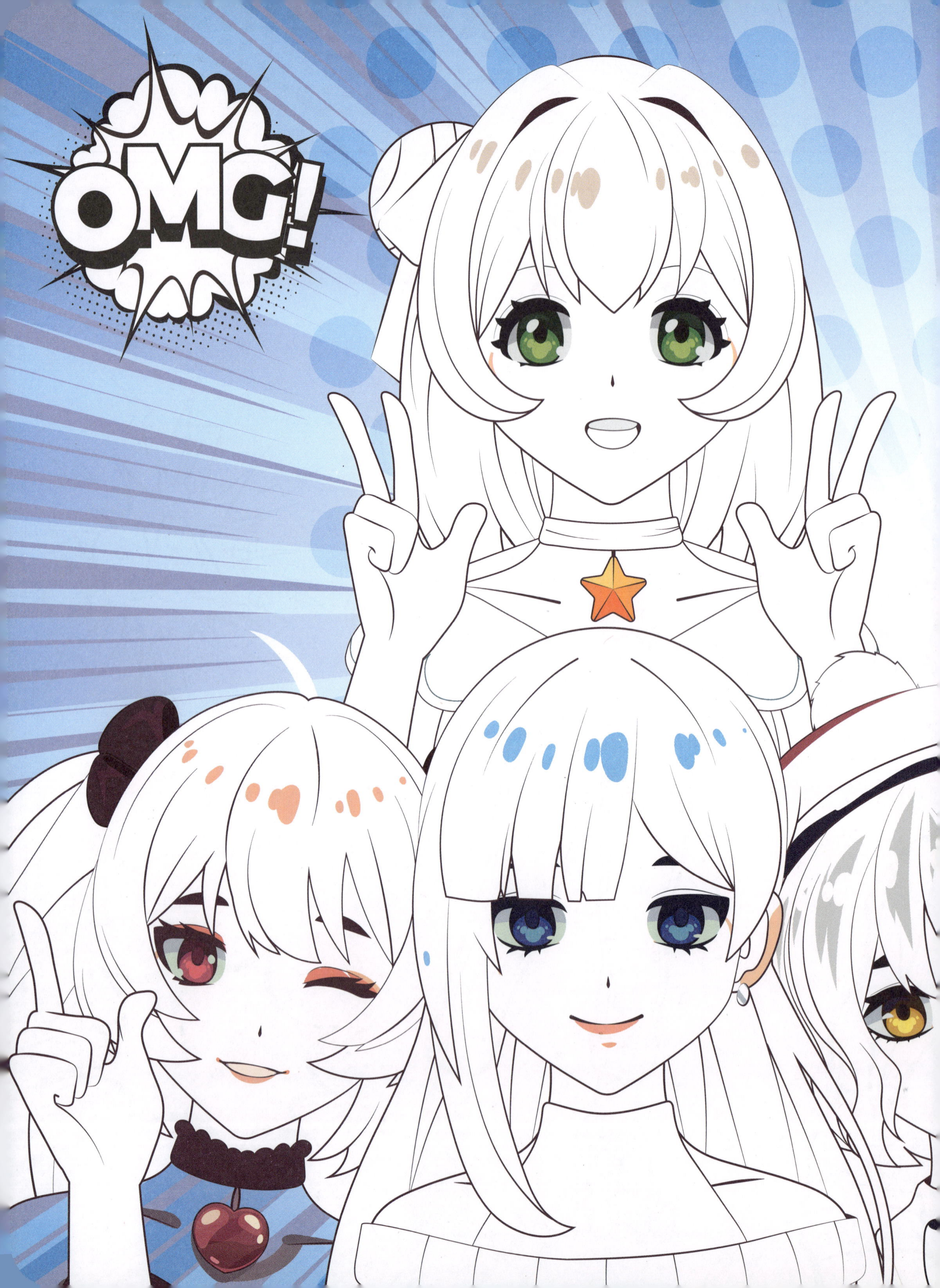
OMG!

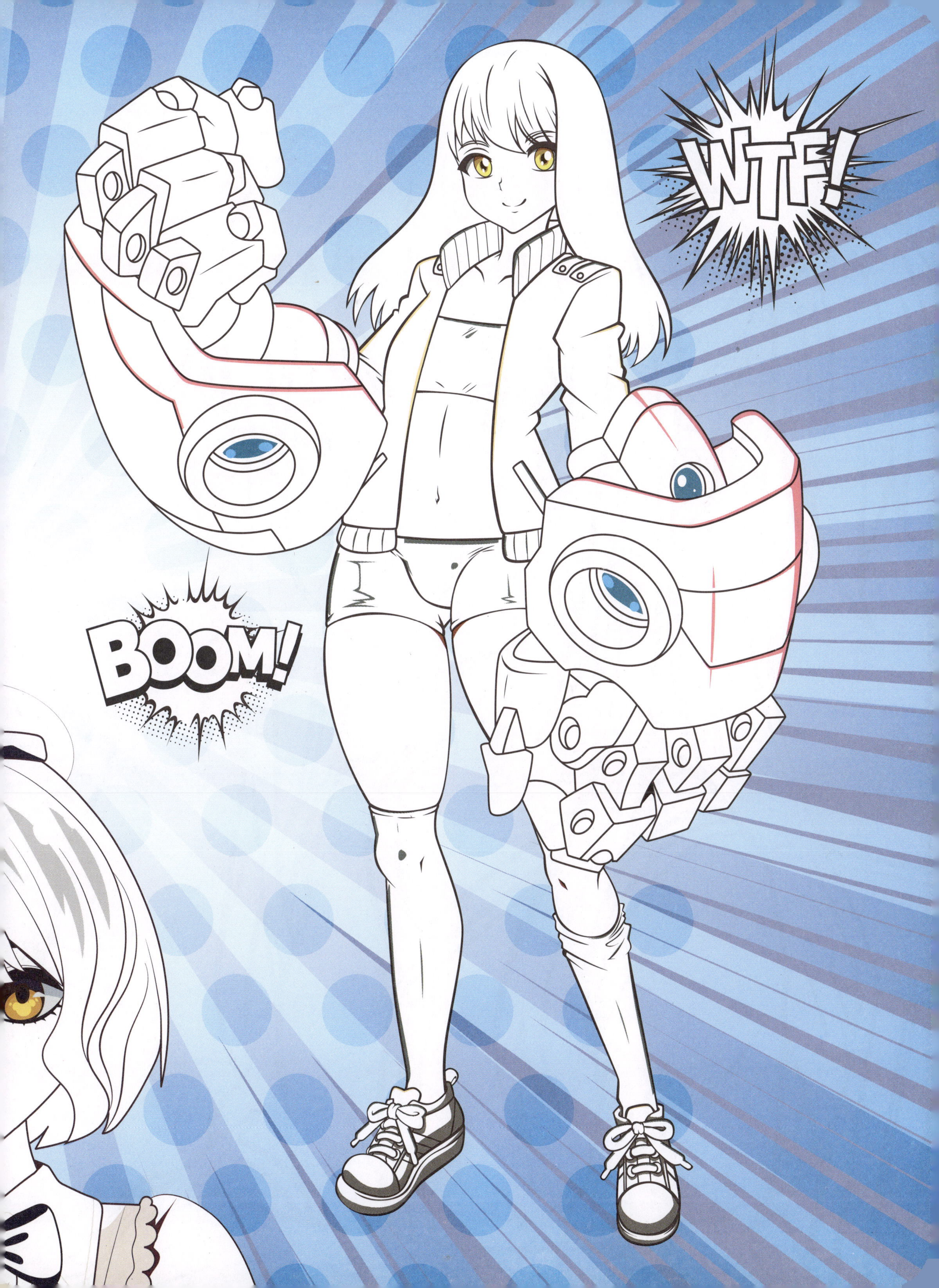
WTF!
BOOM!

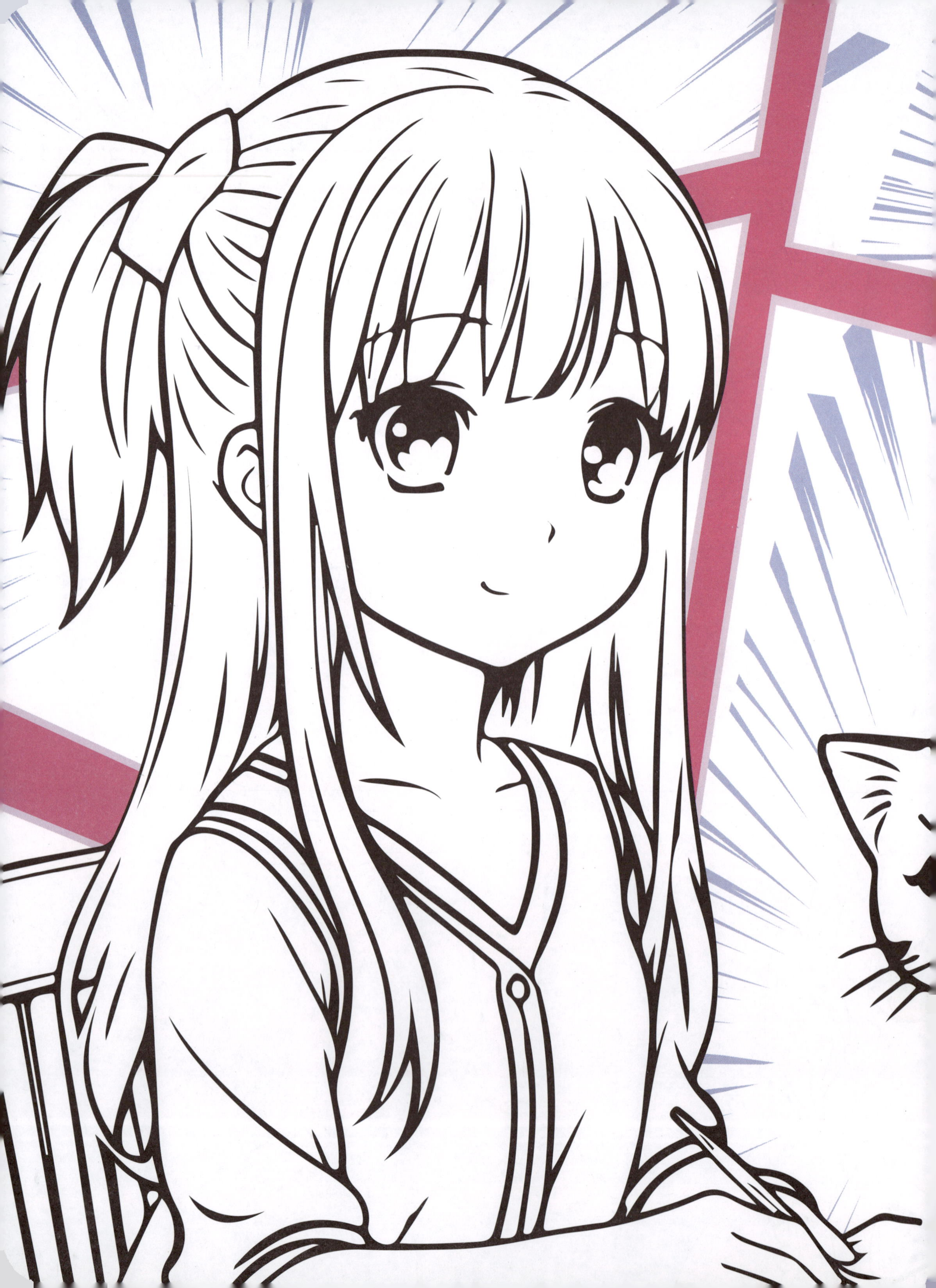

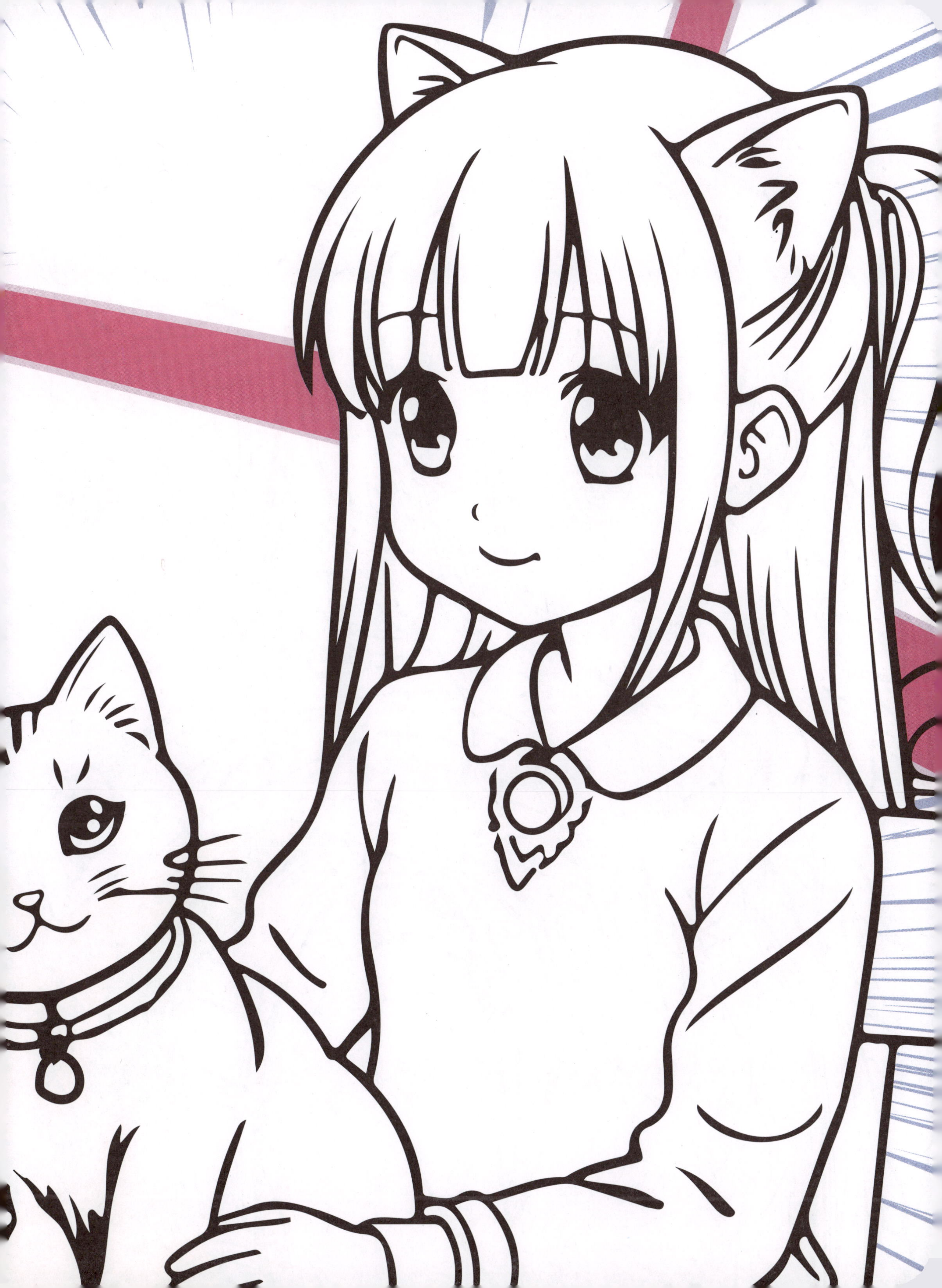

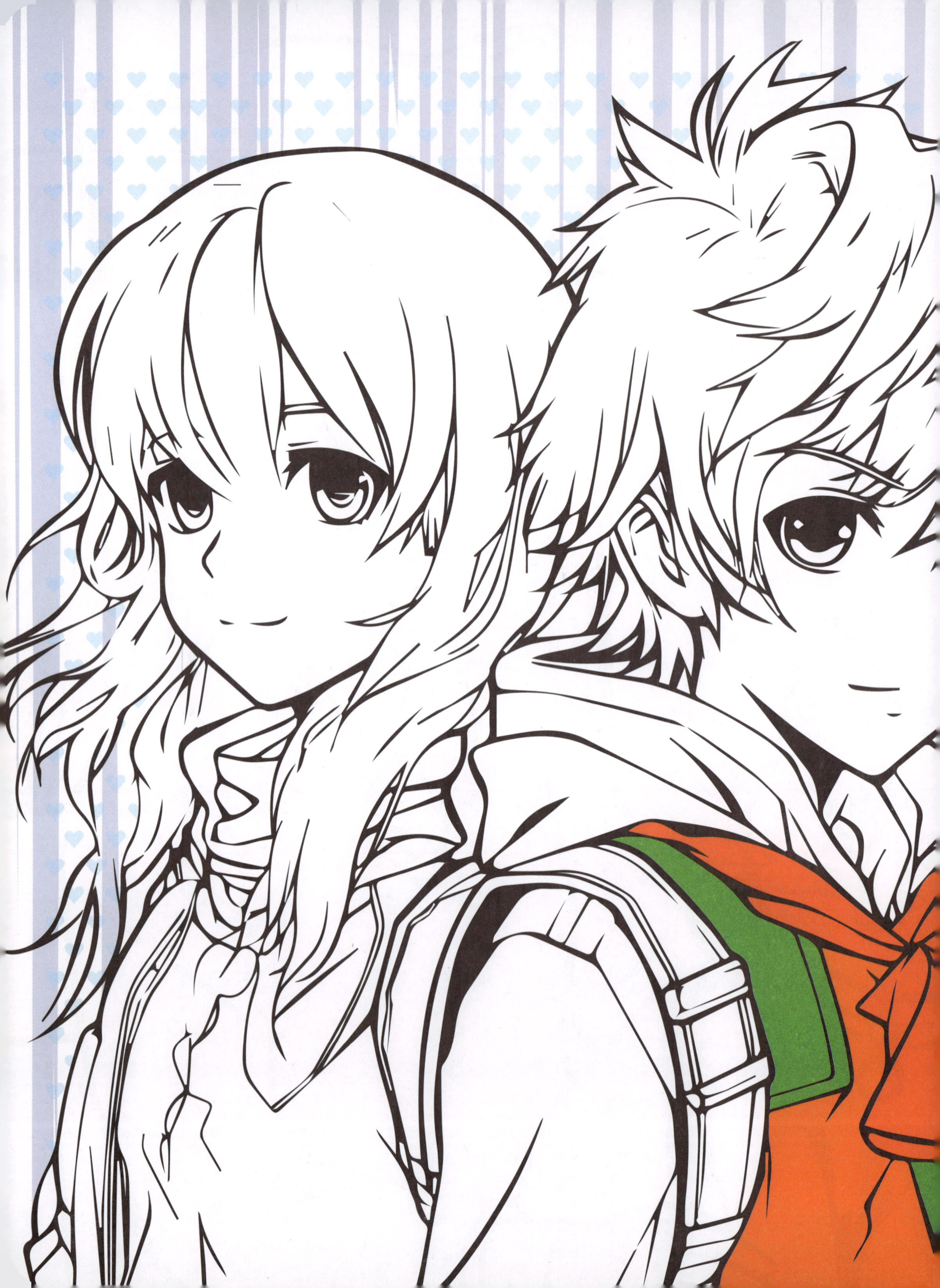

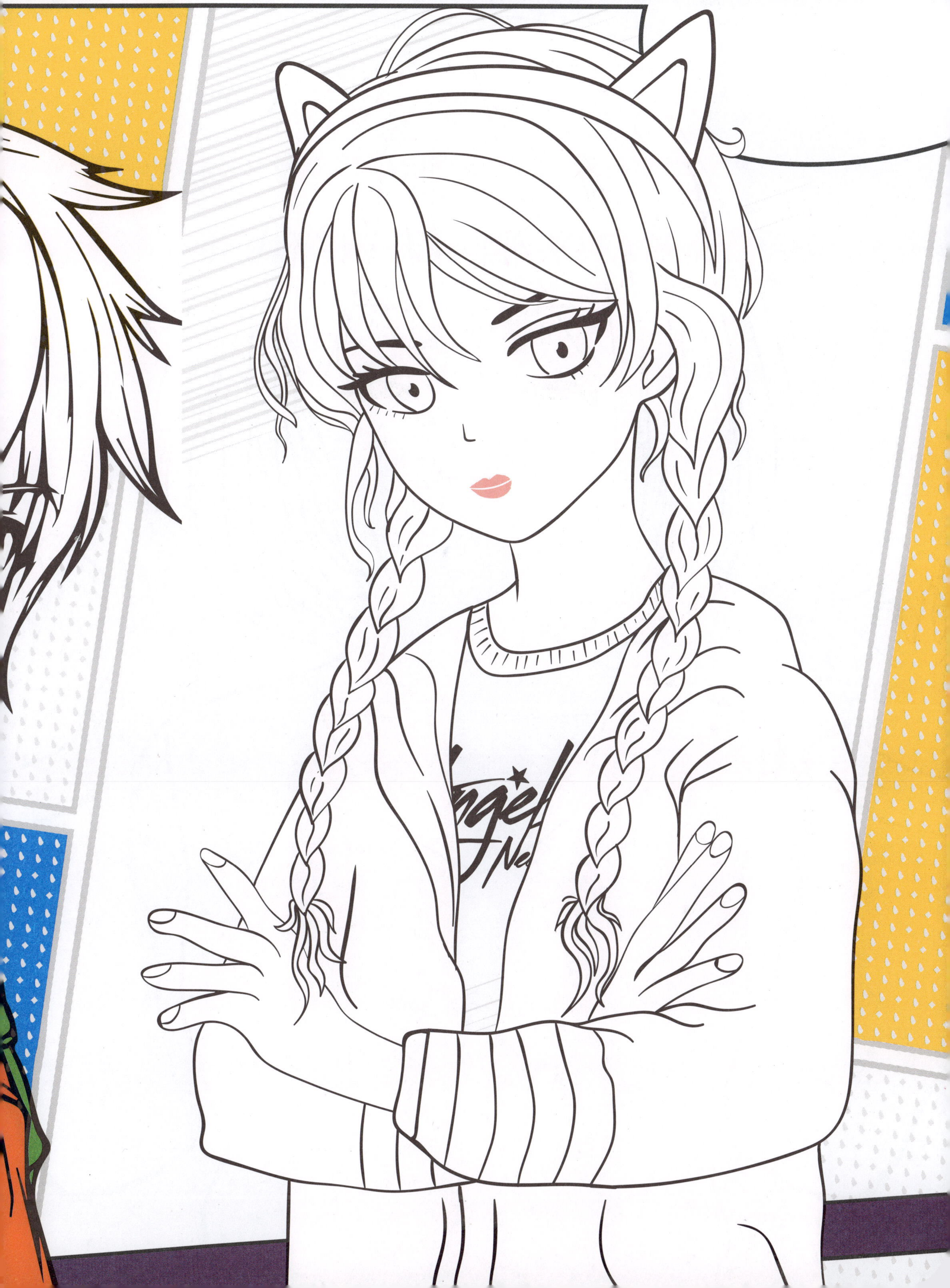

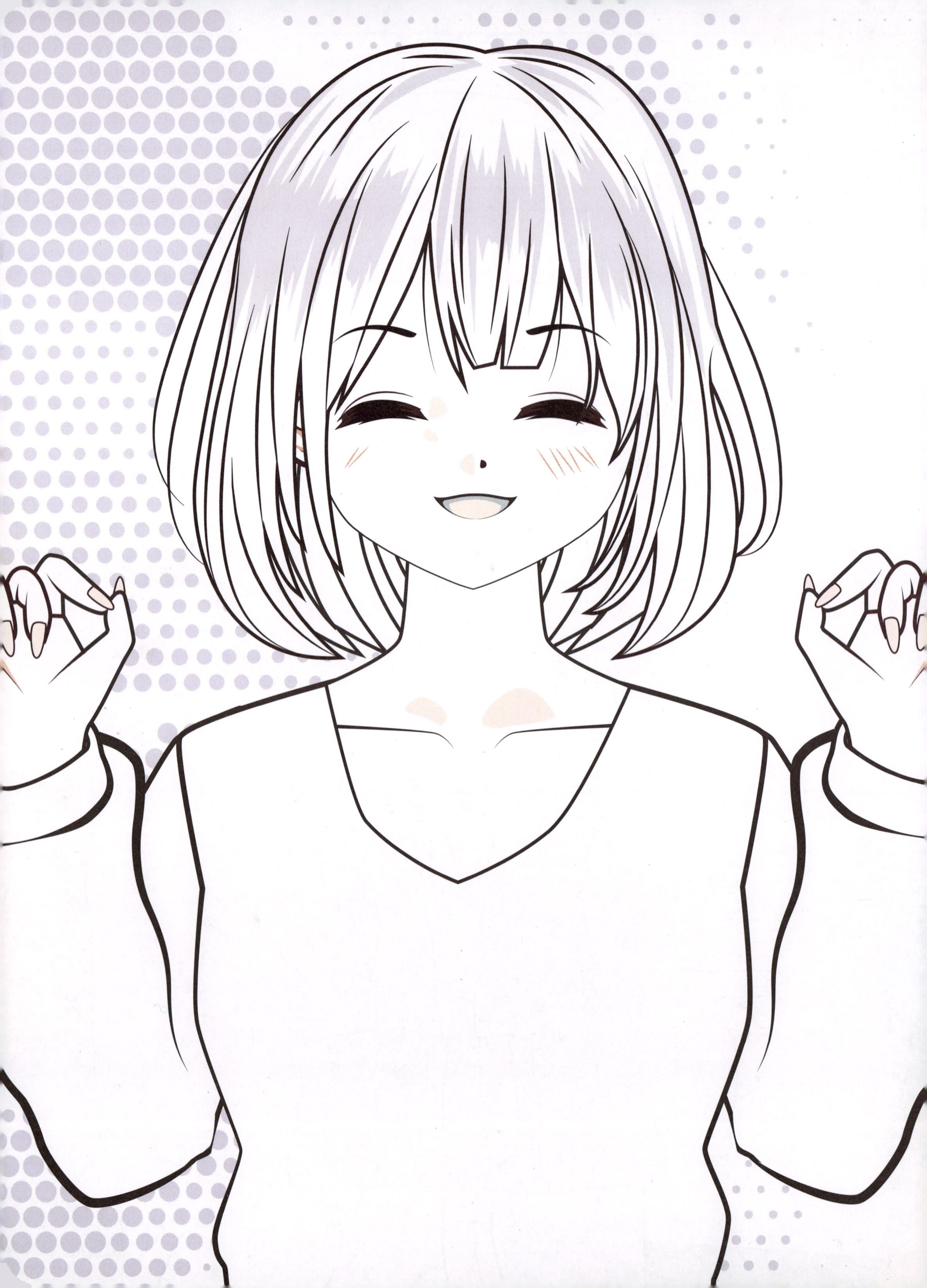

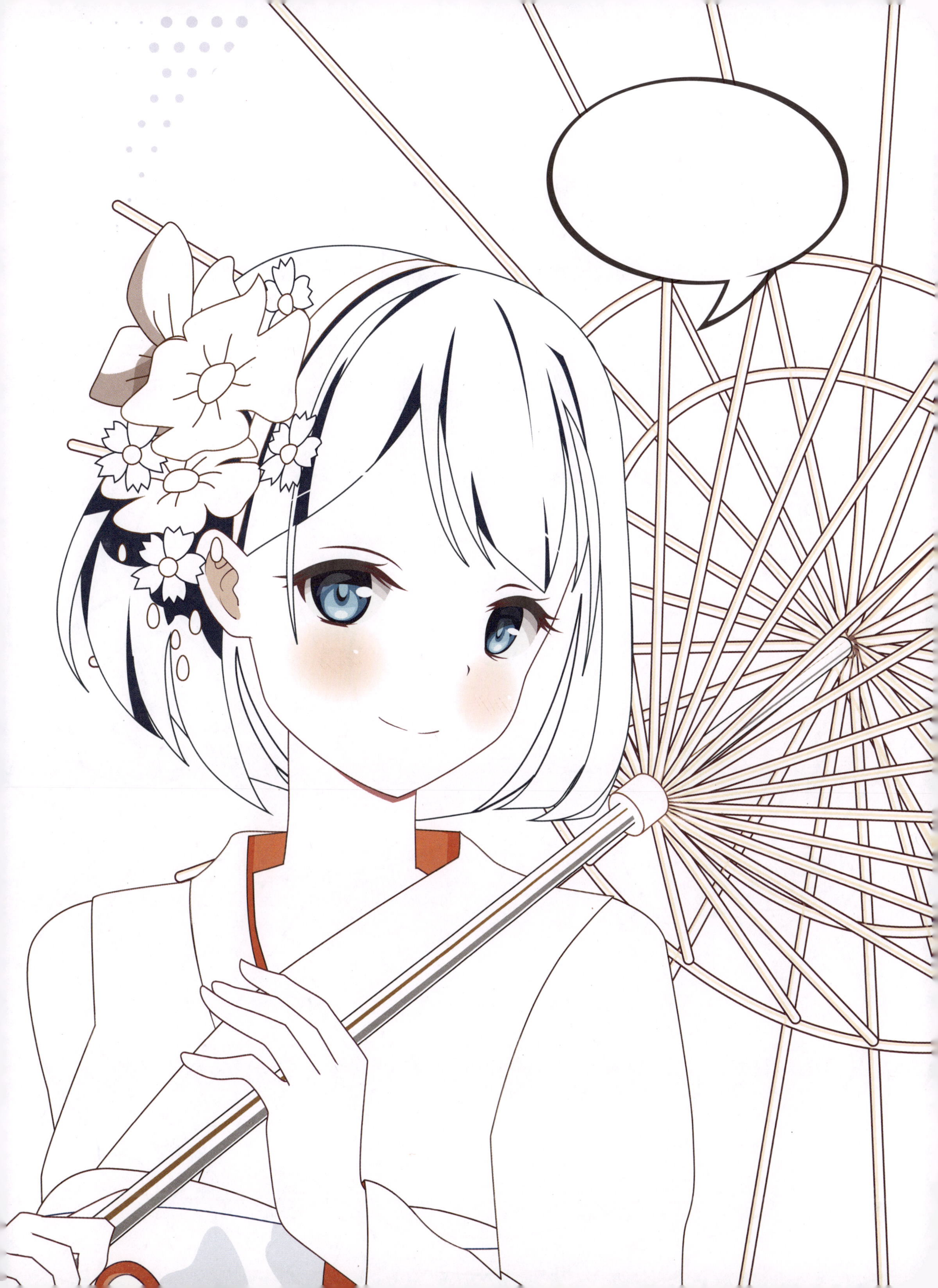

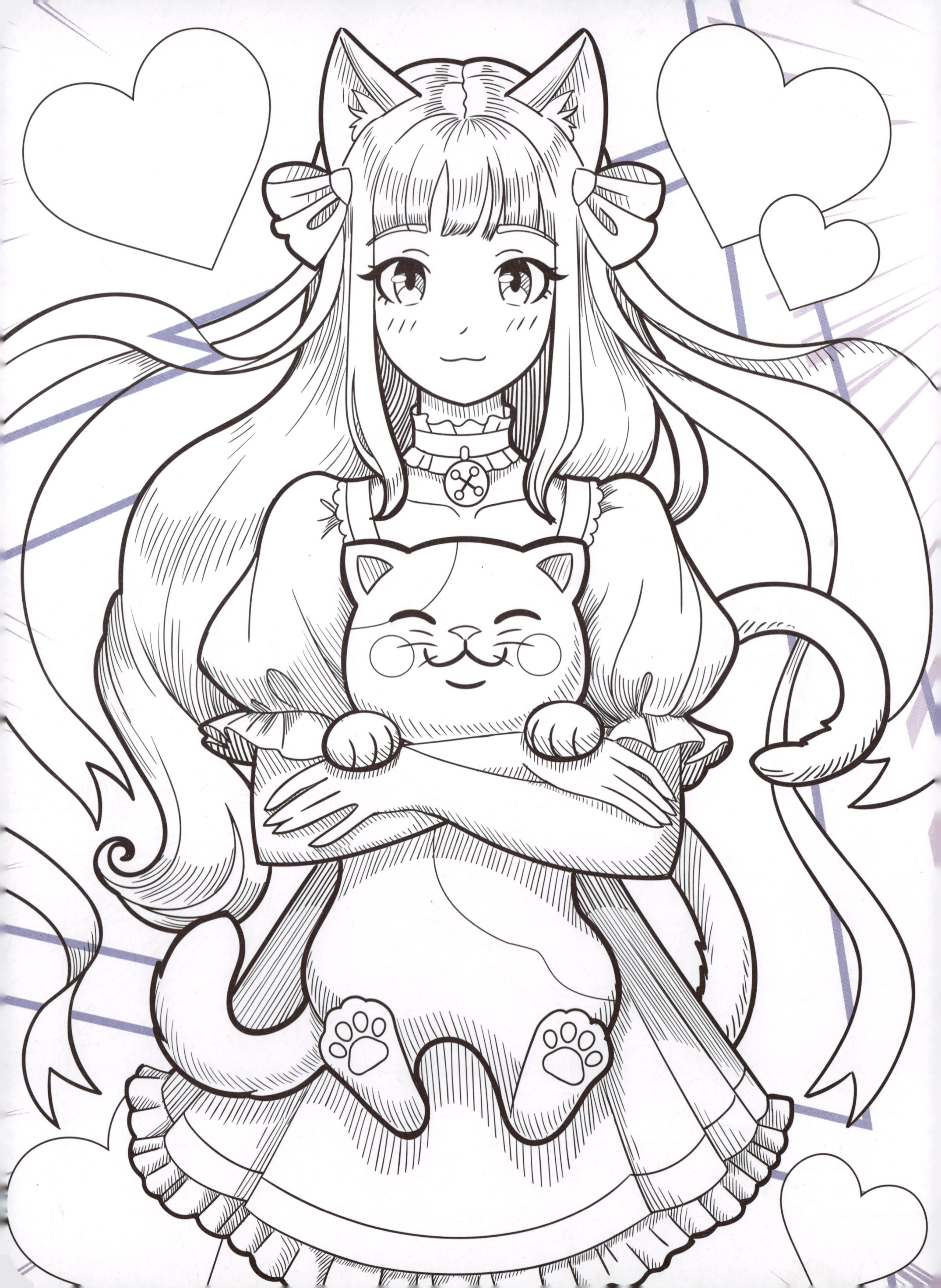

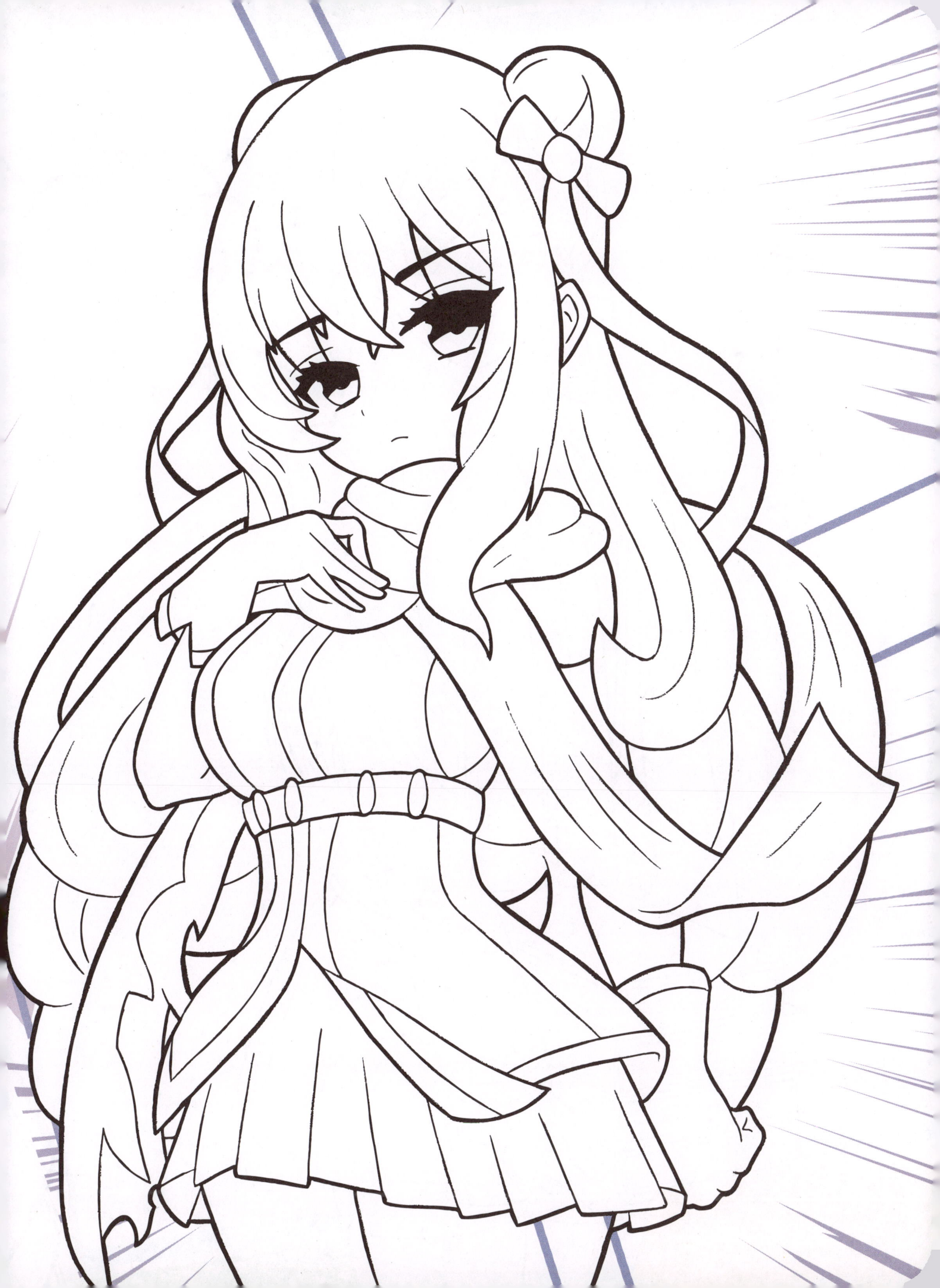

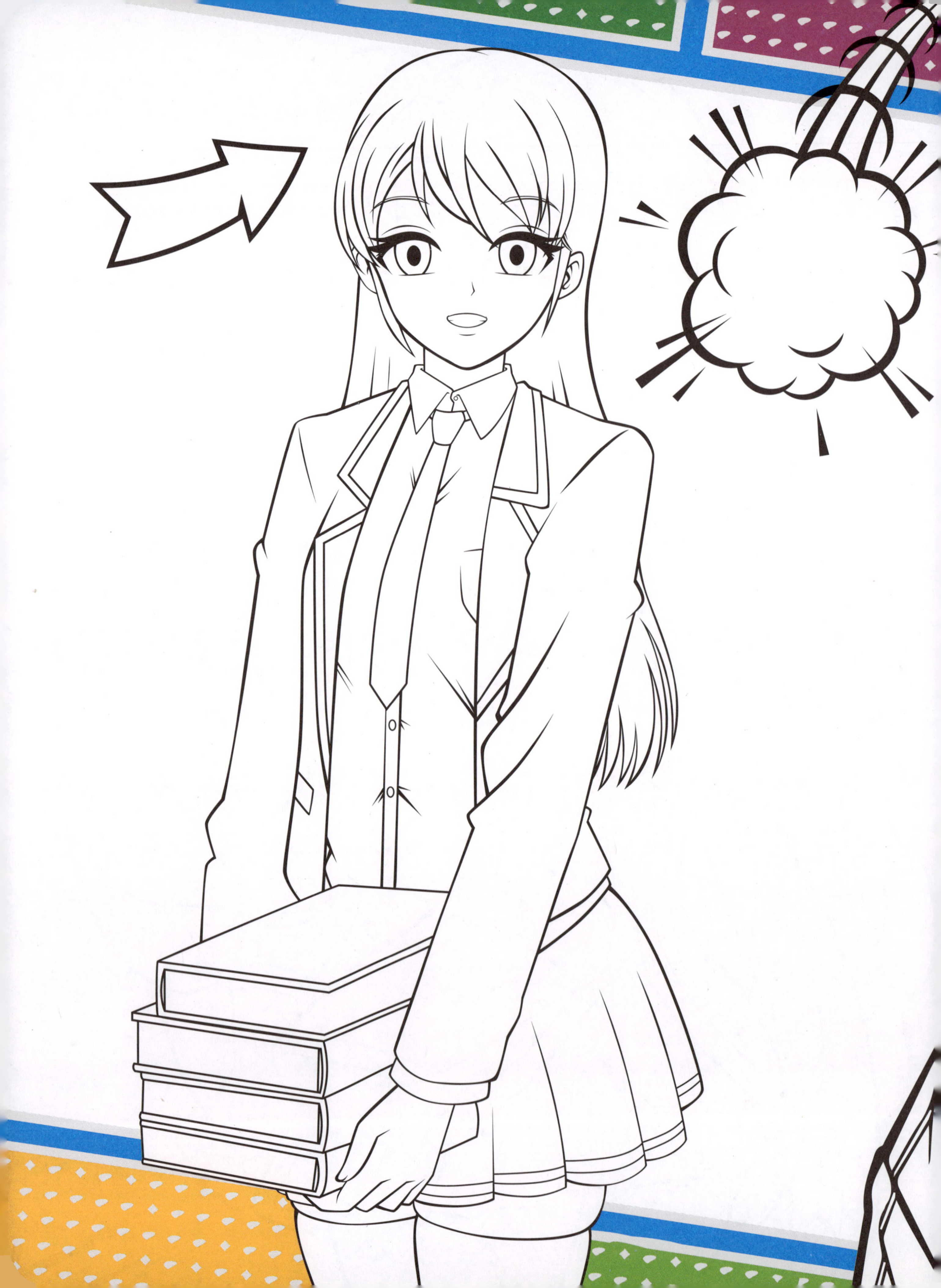

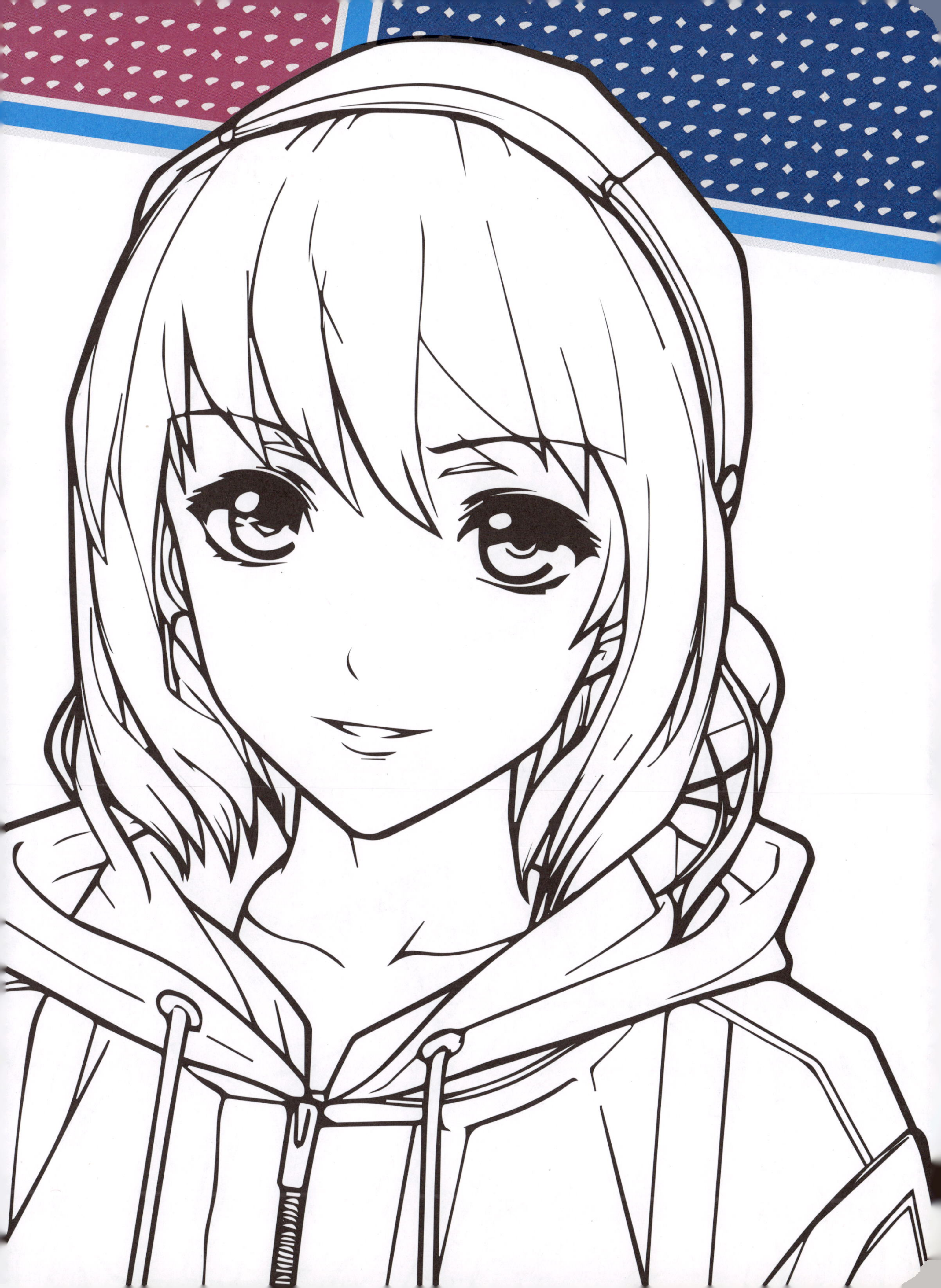

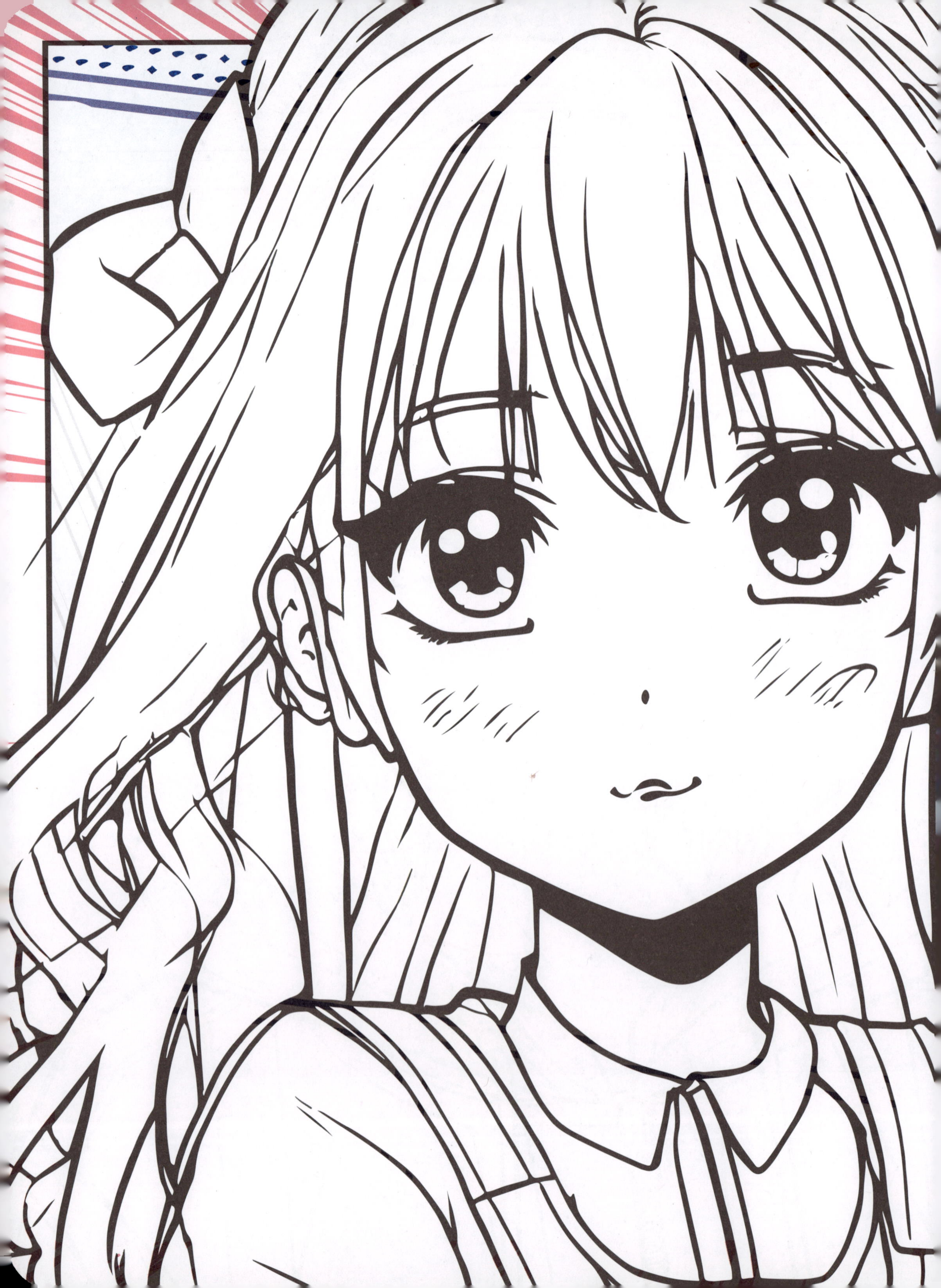

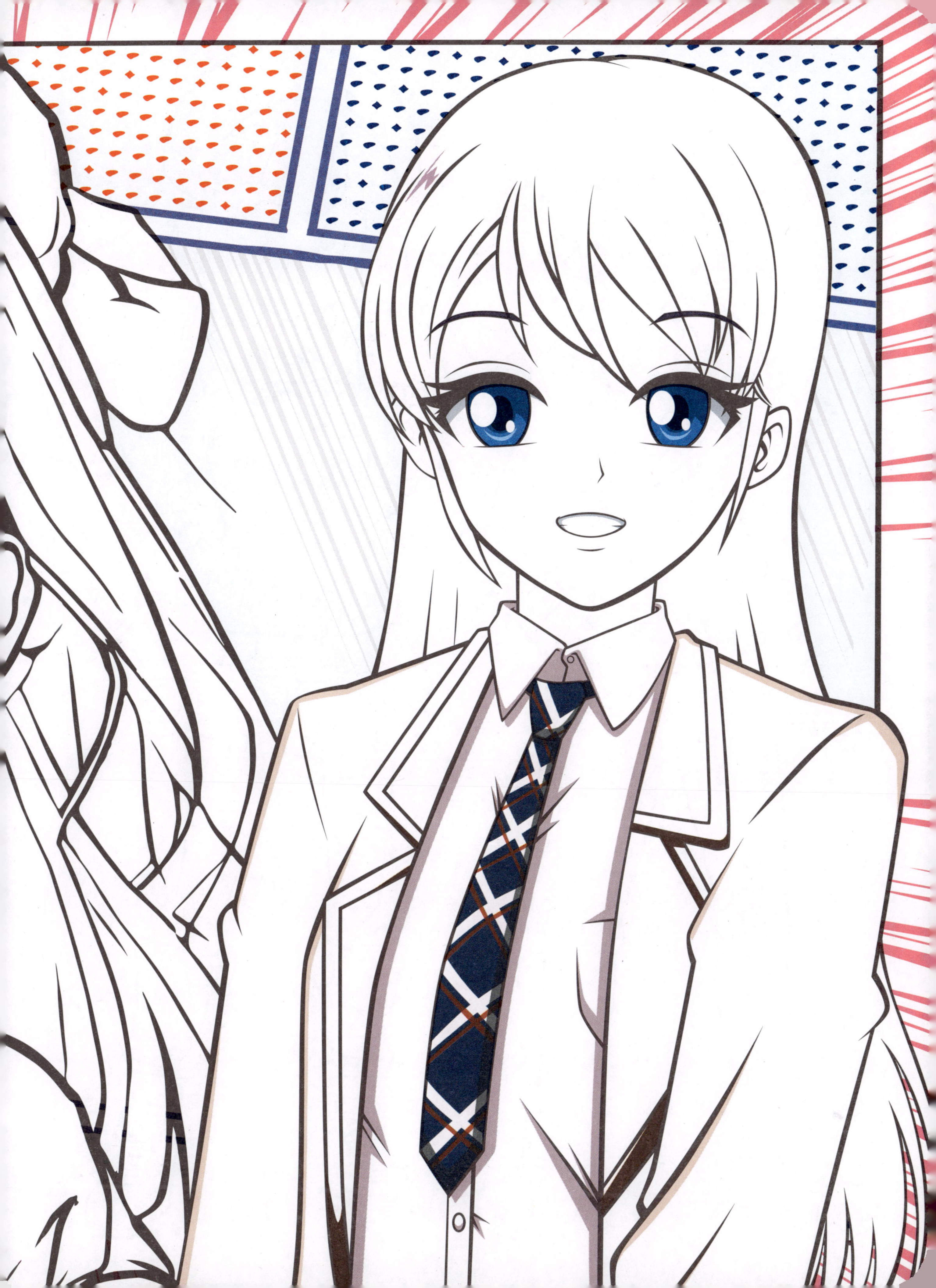

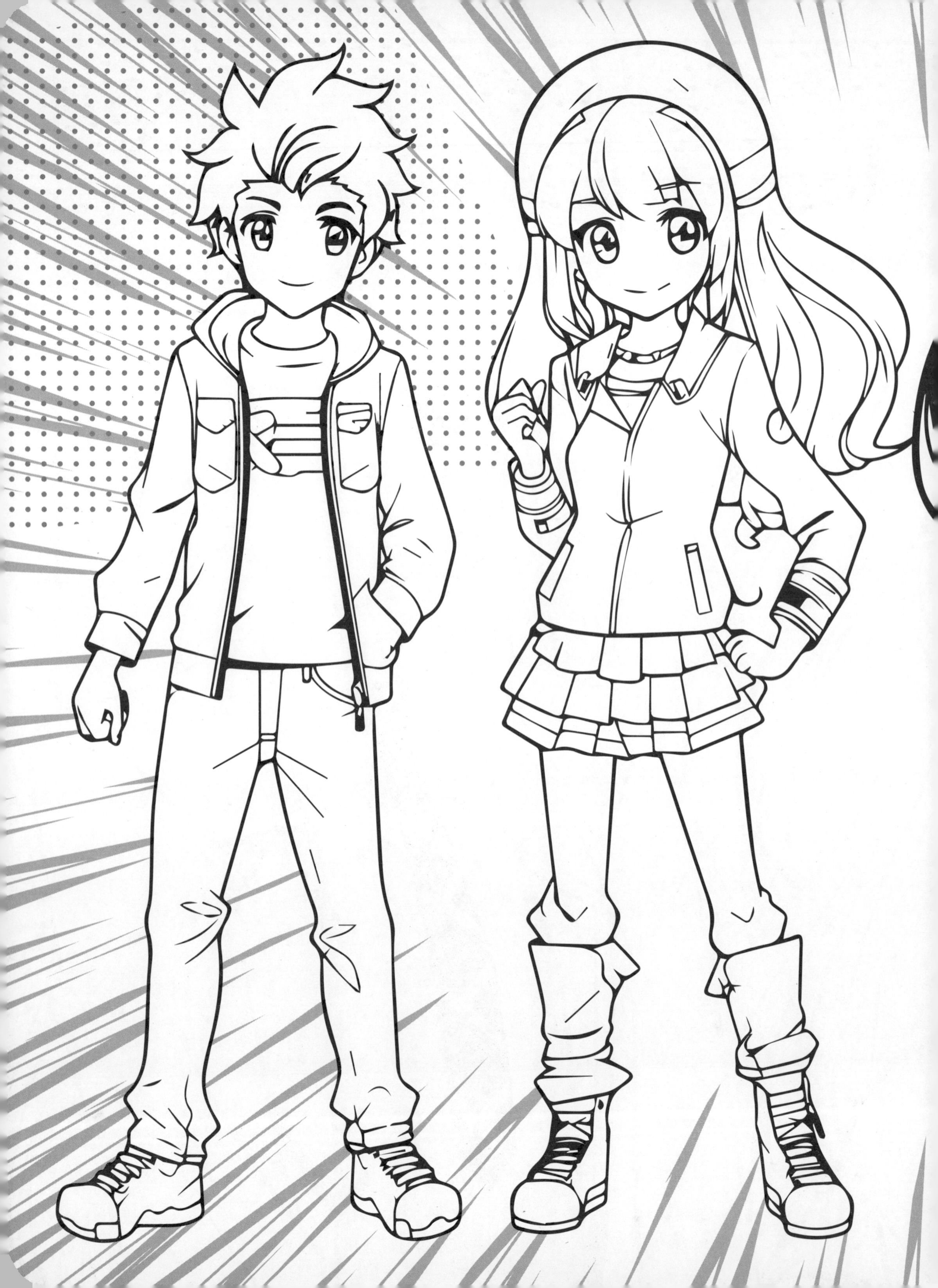

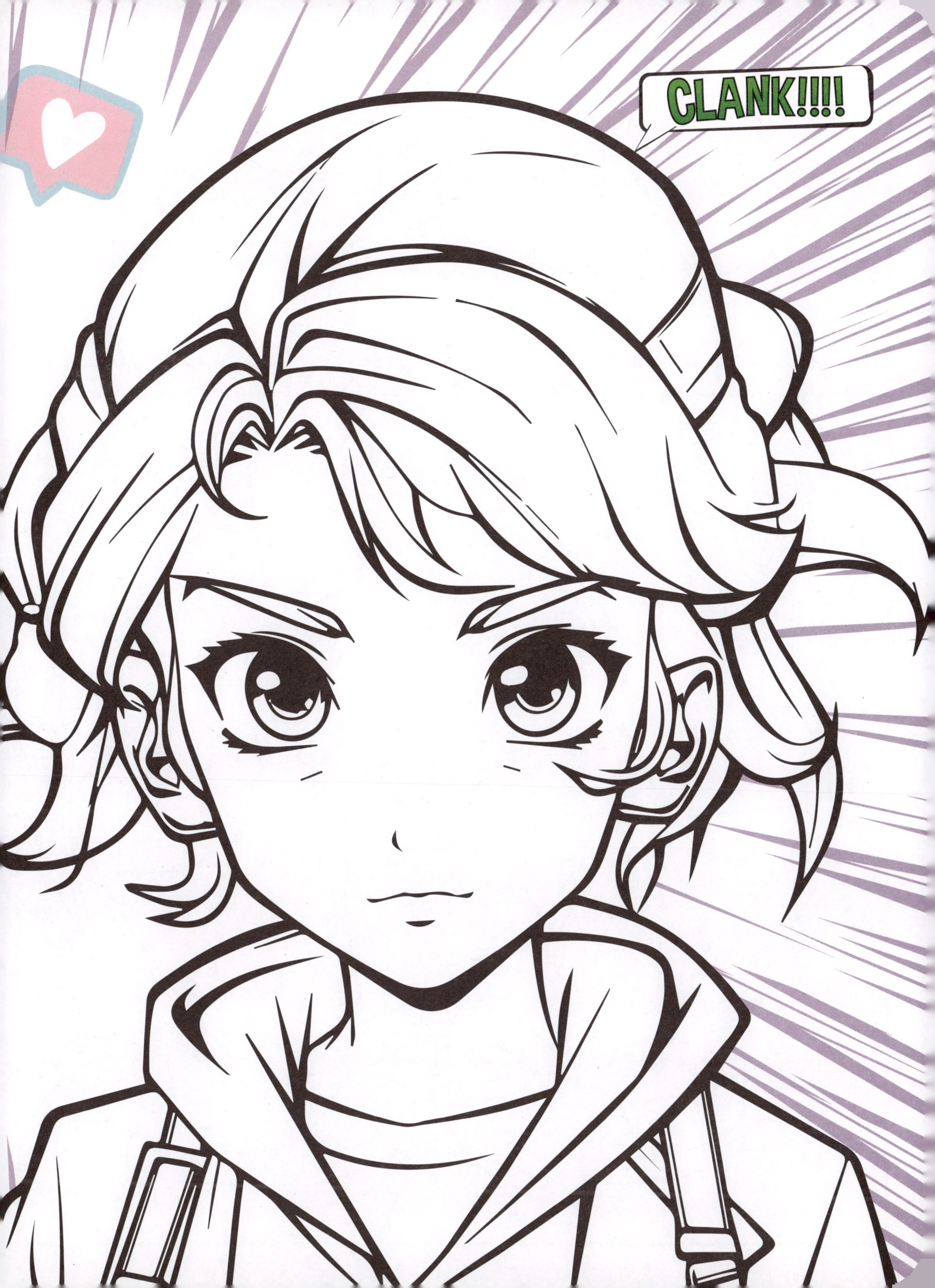
CLANK!!!!

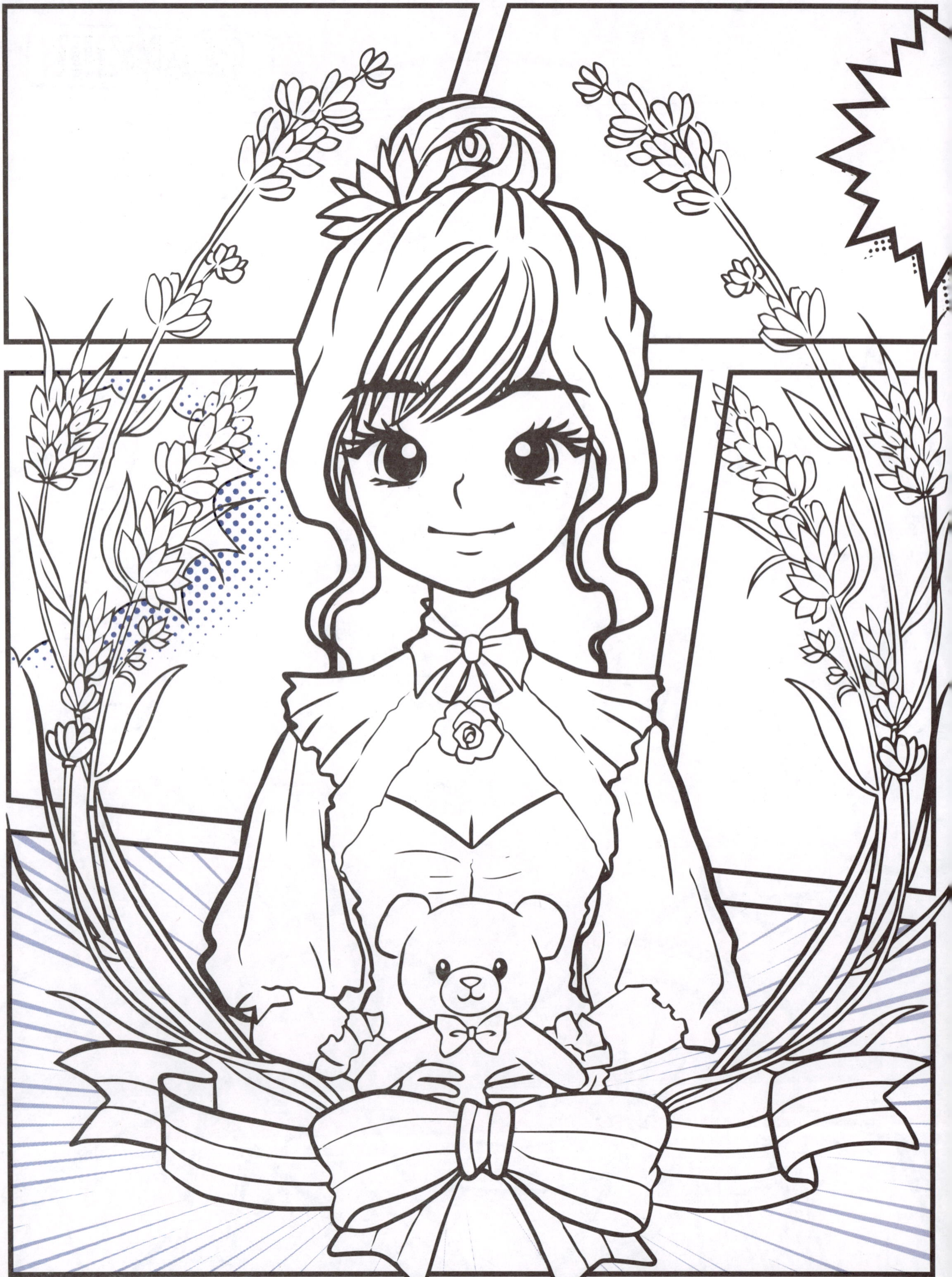

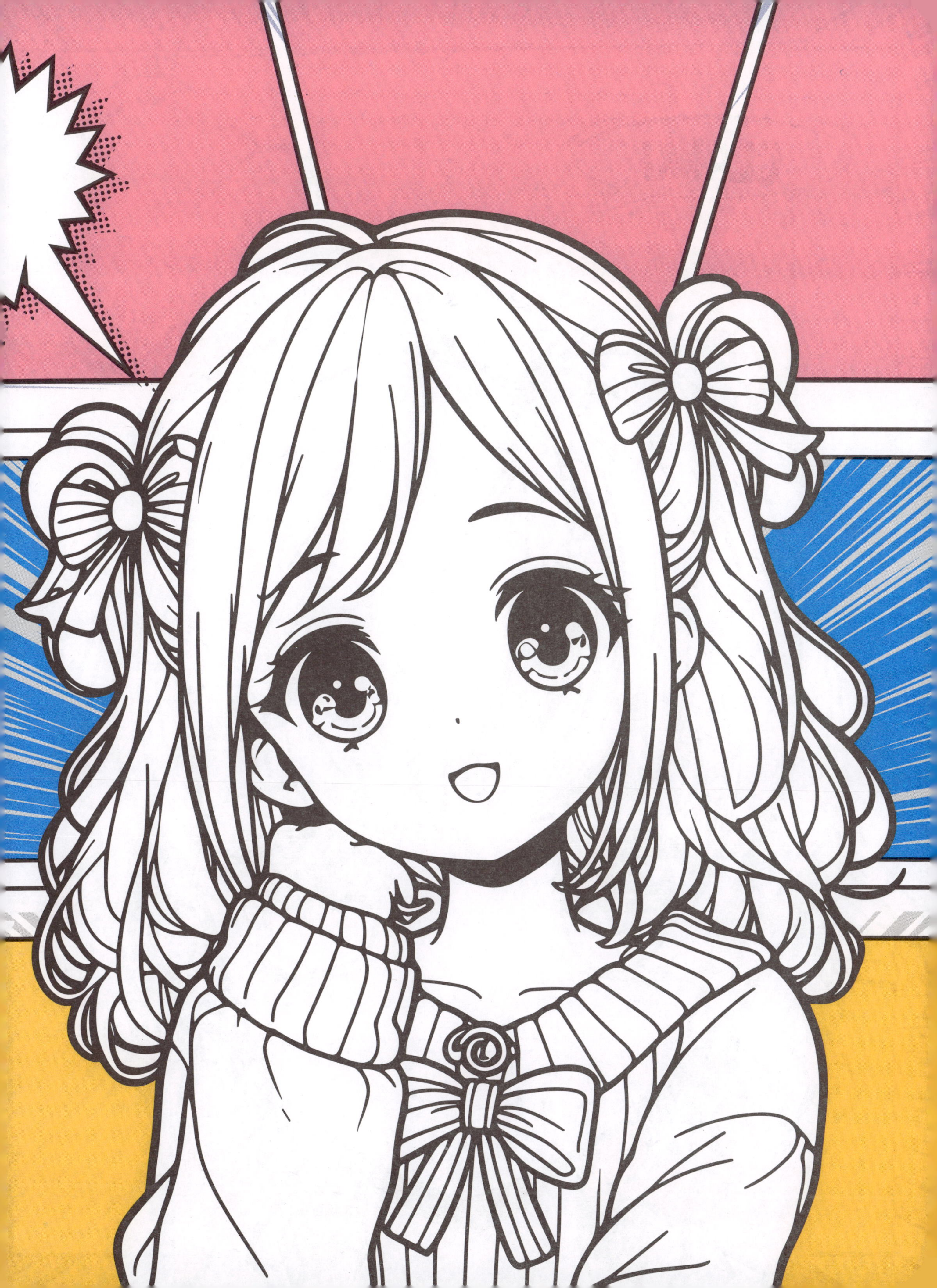

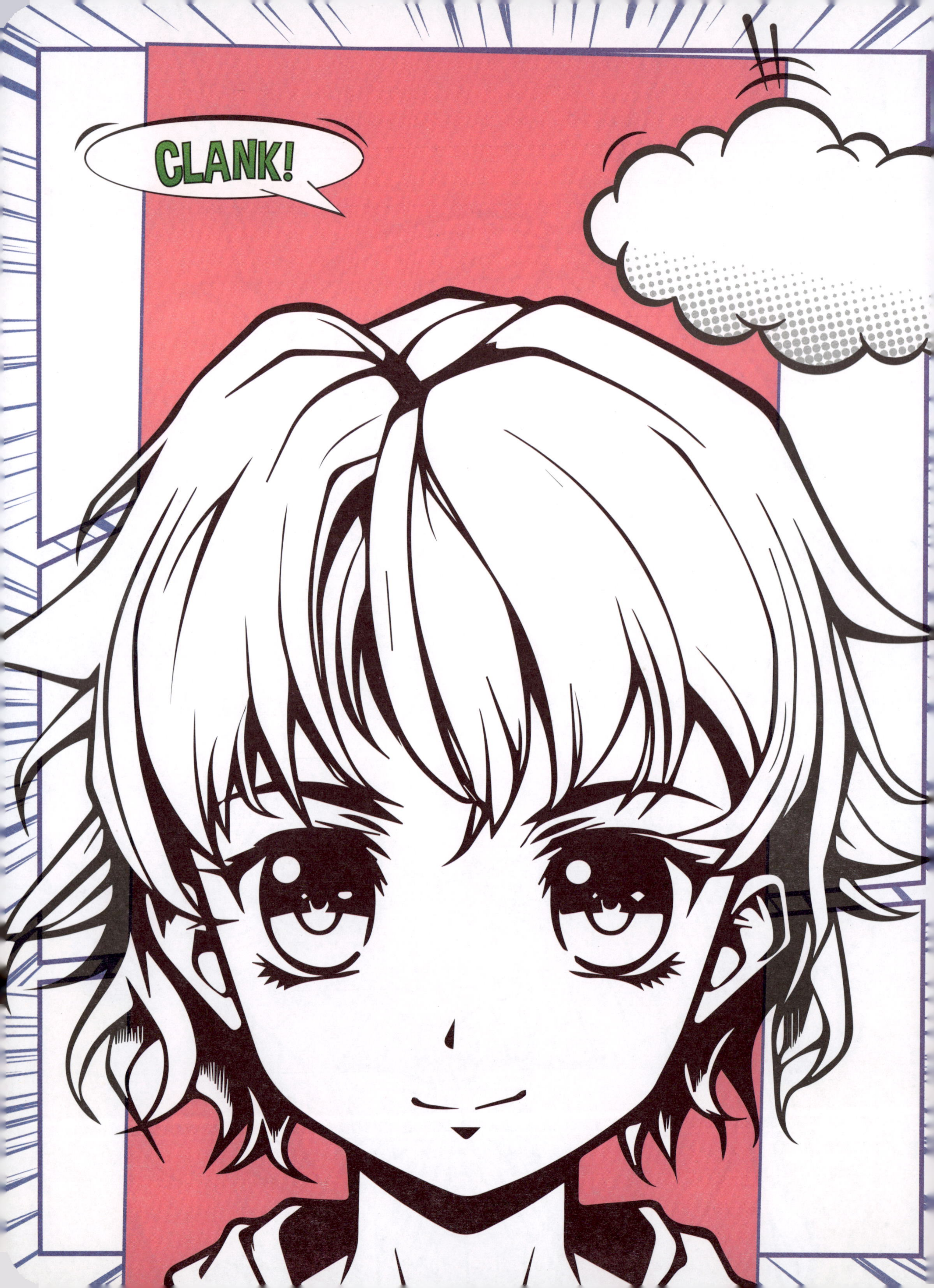
CLANK!

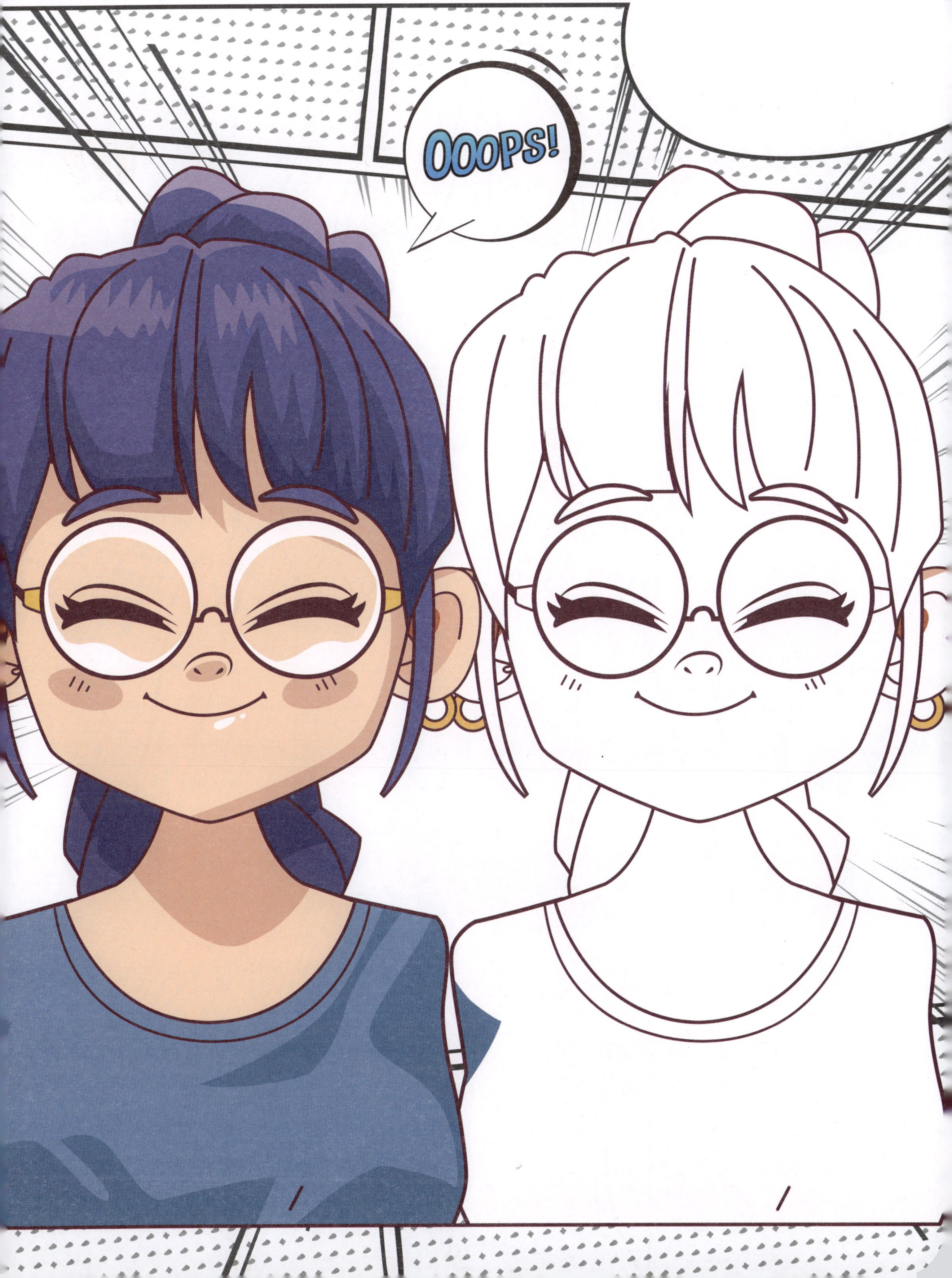
OOOPS!

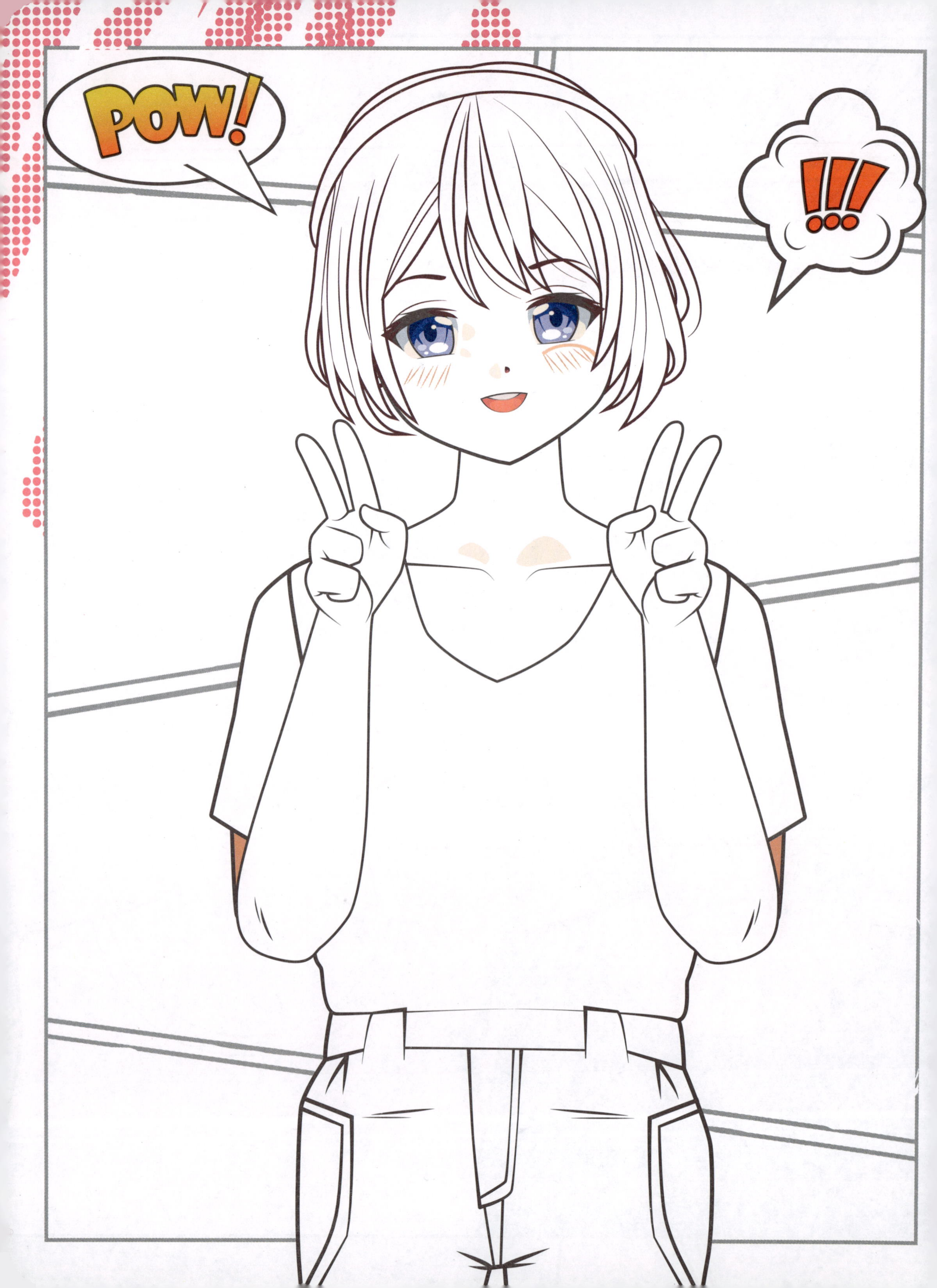
POW!
!!!

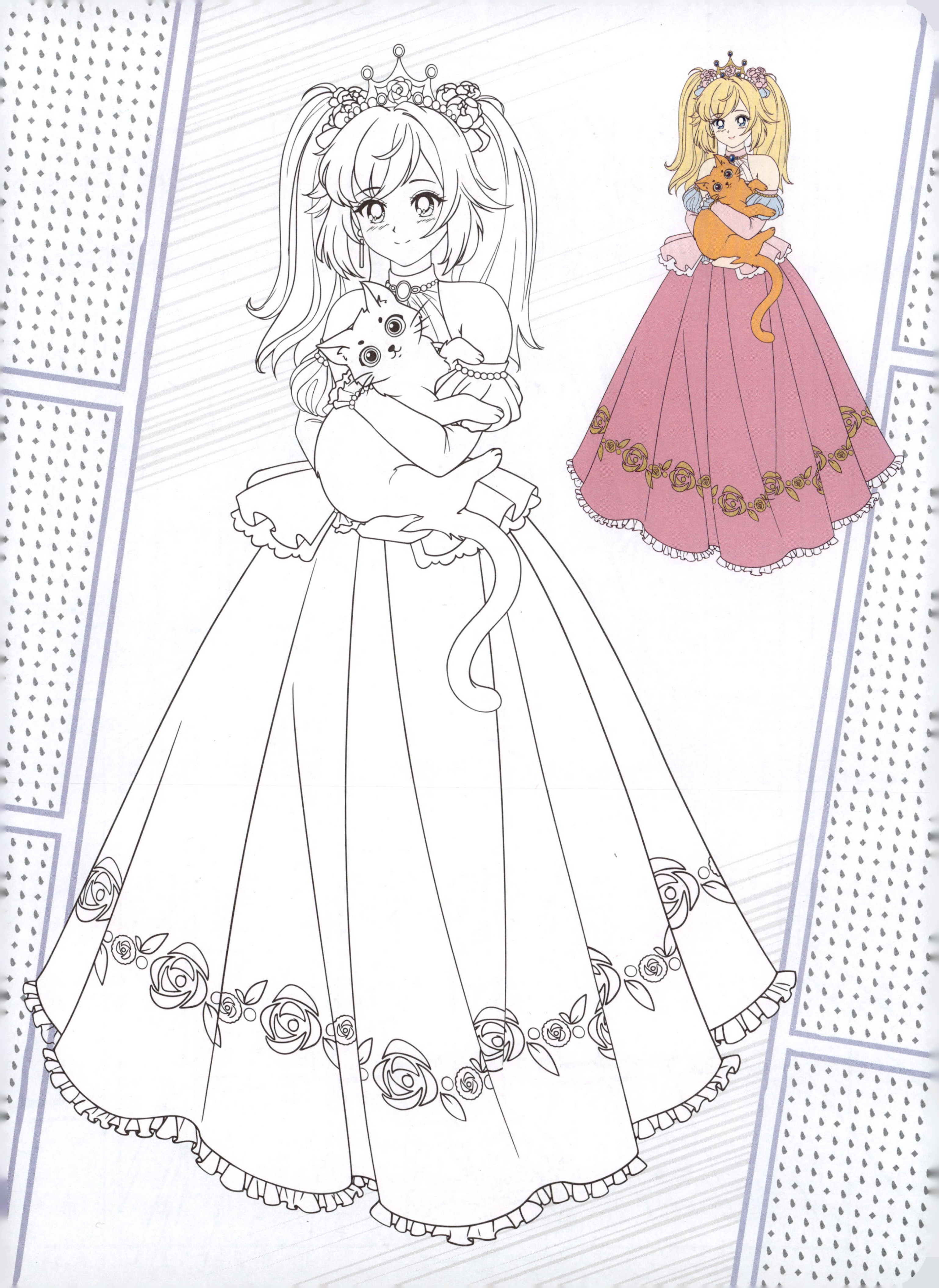

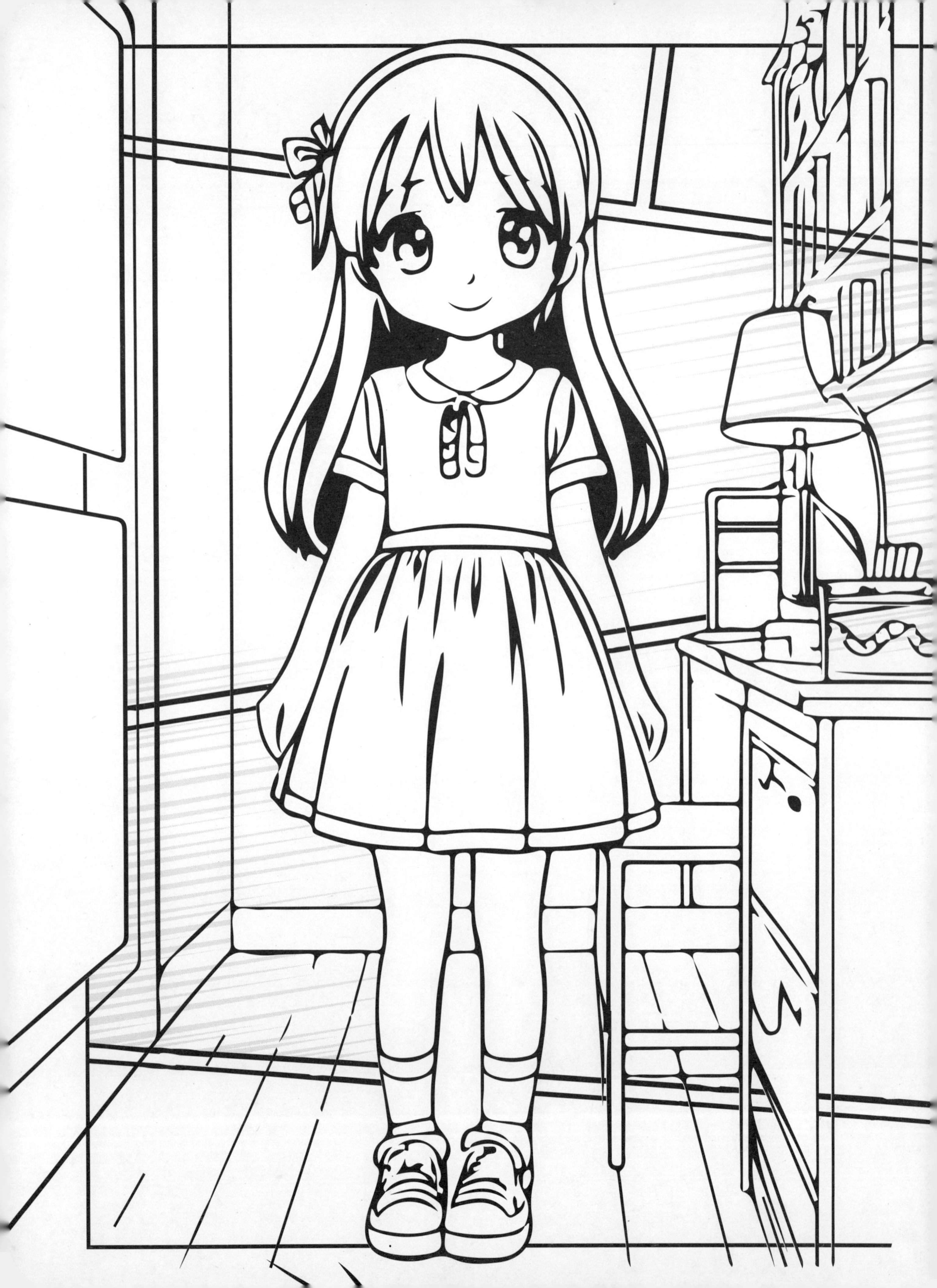

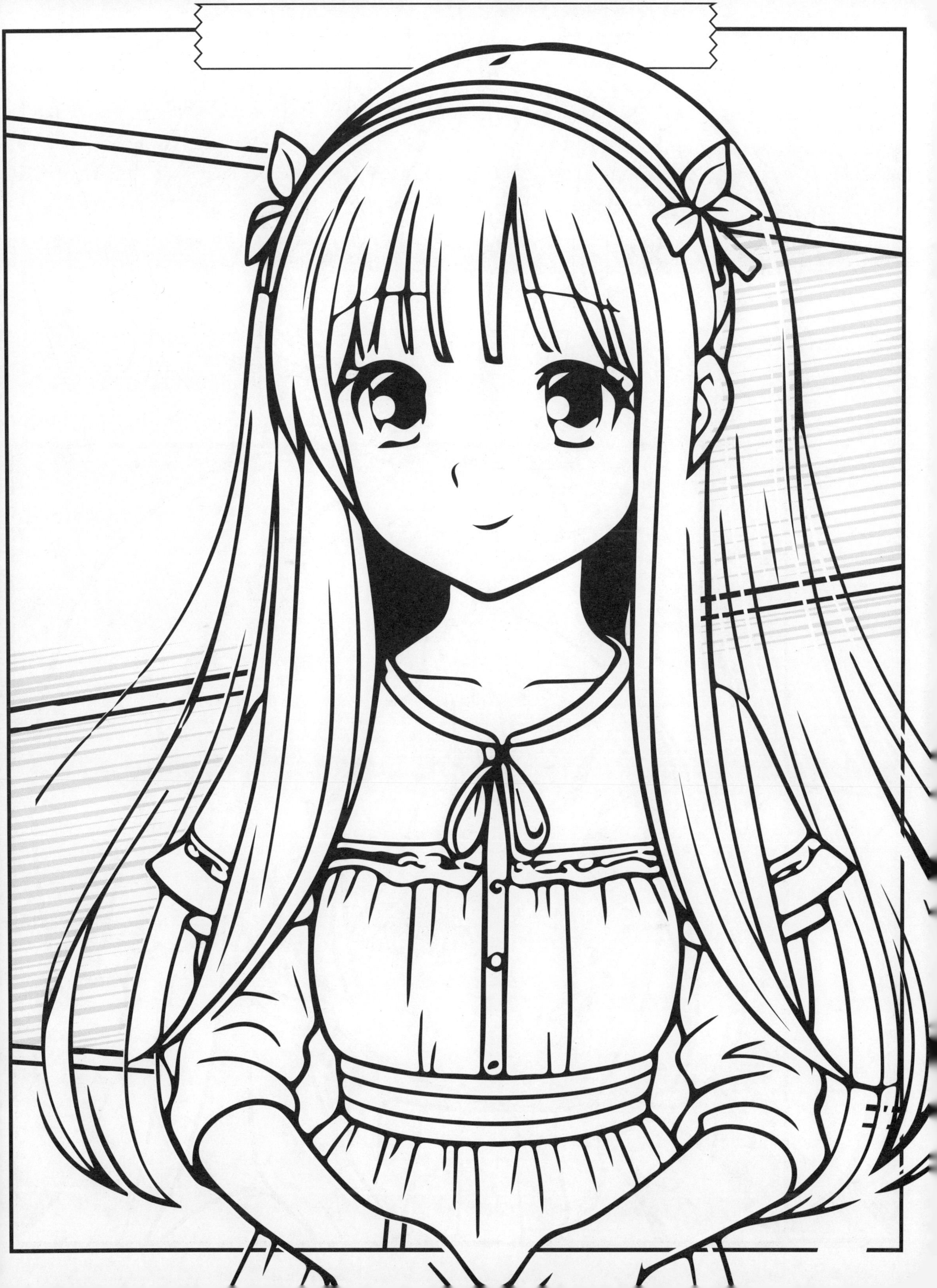

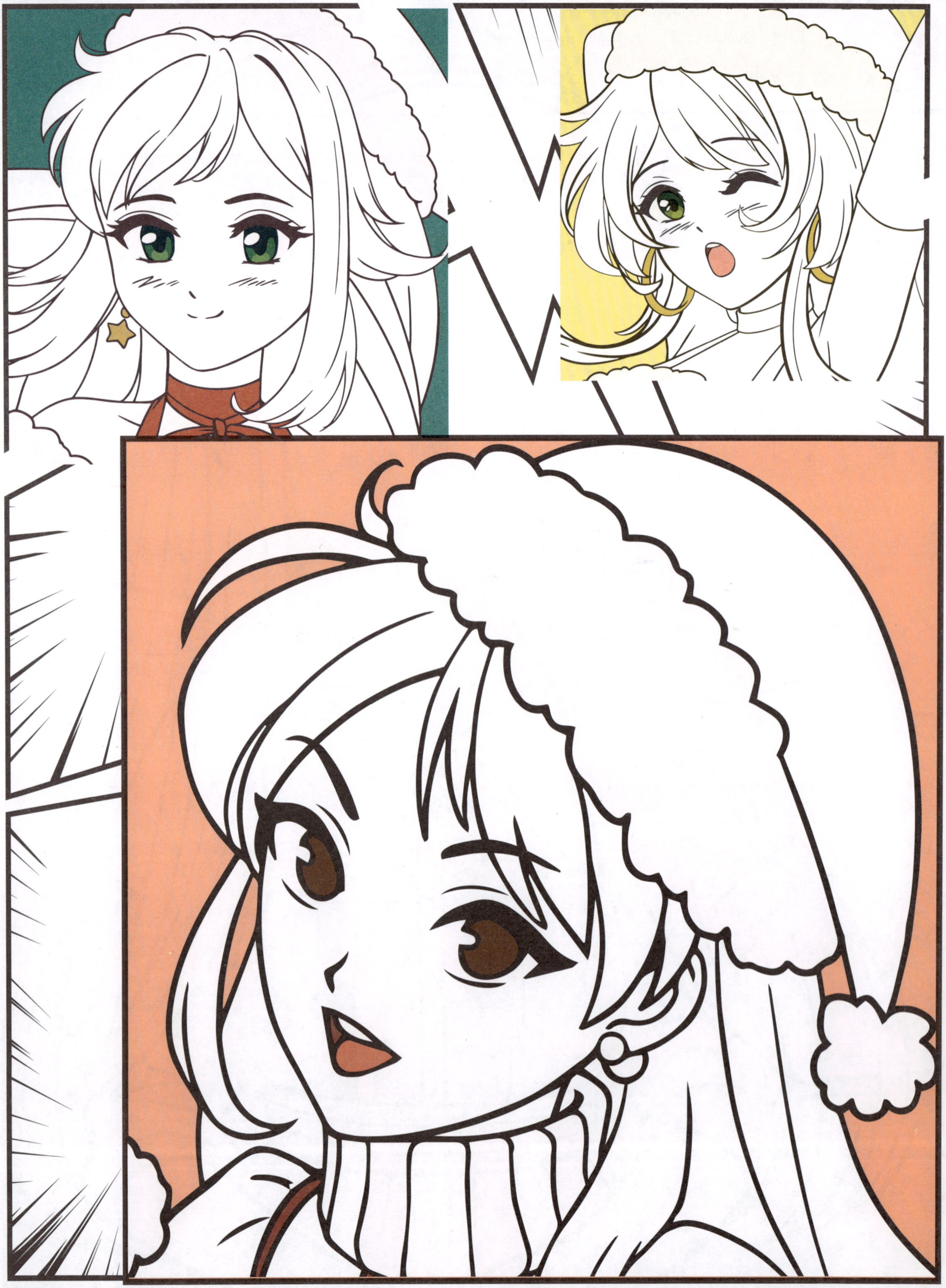

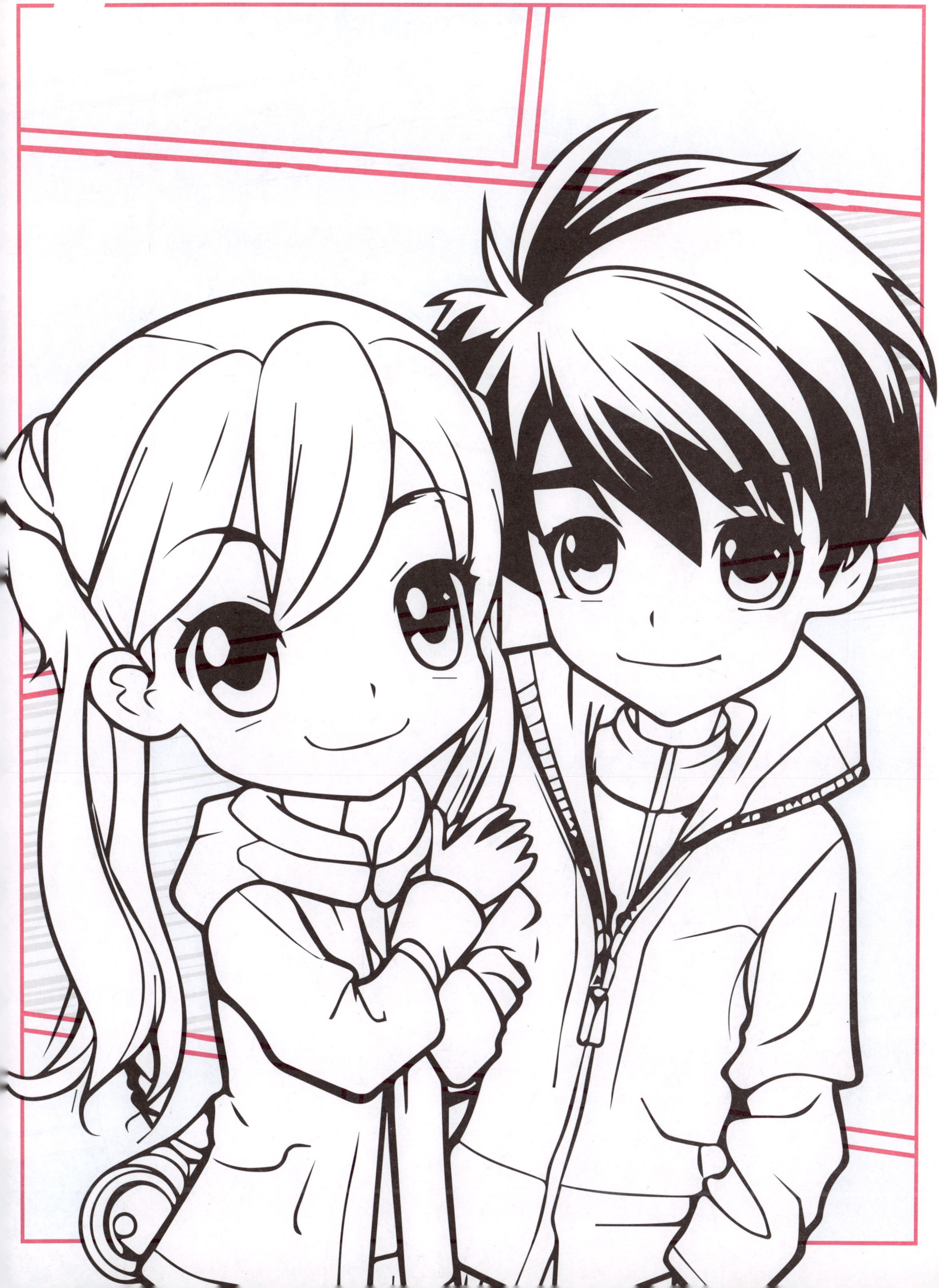

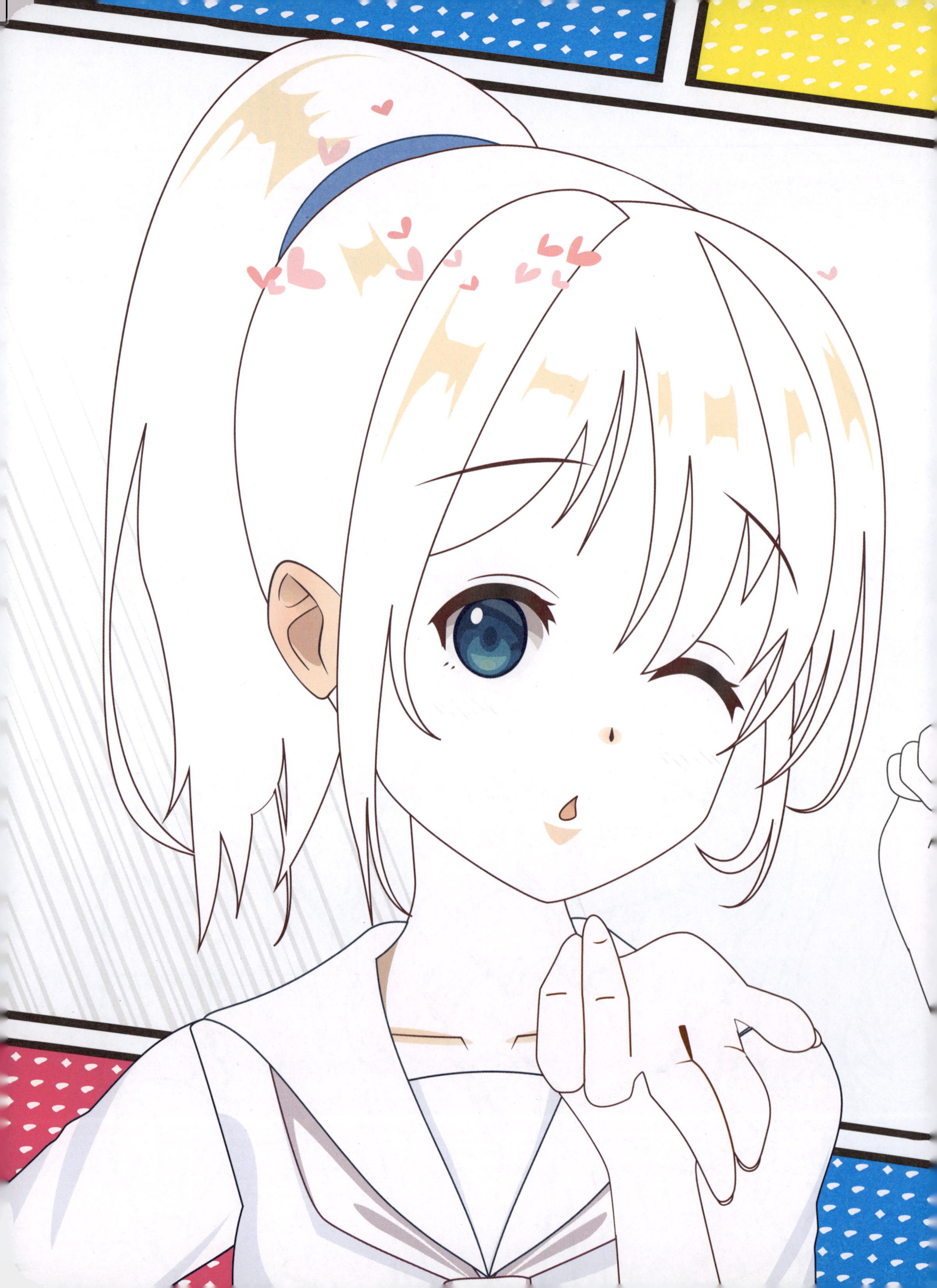

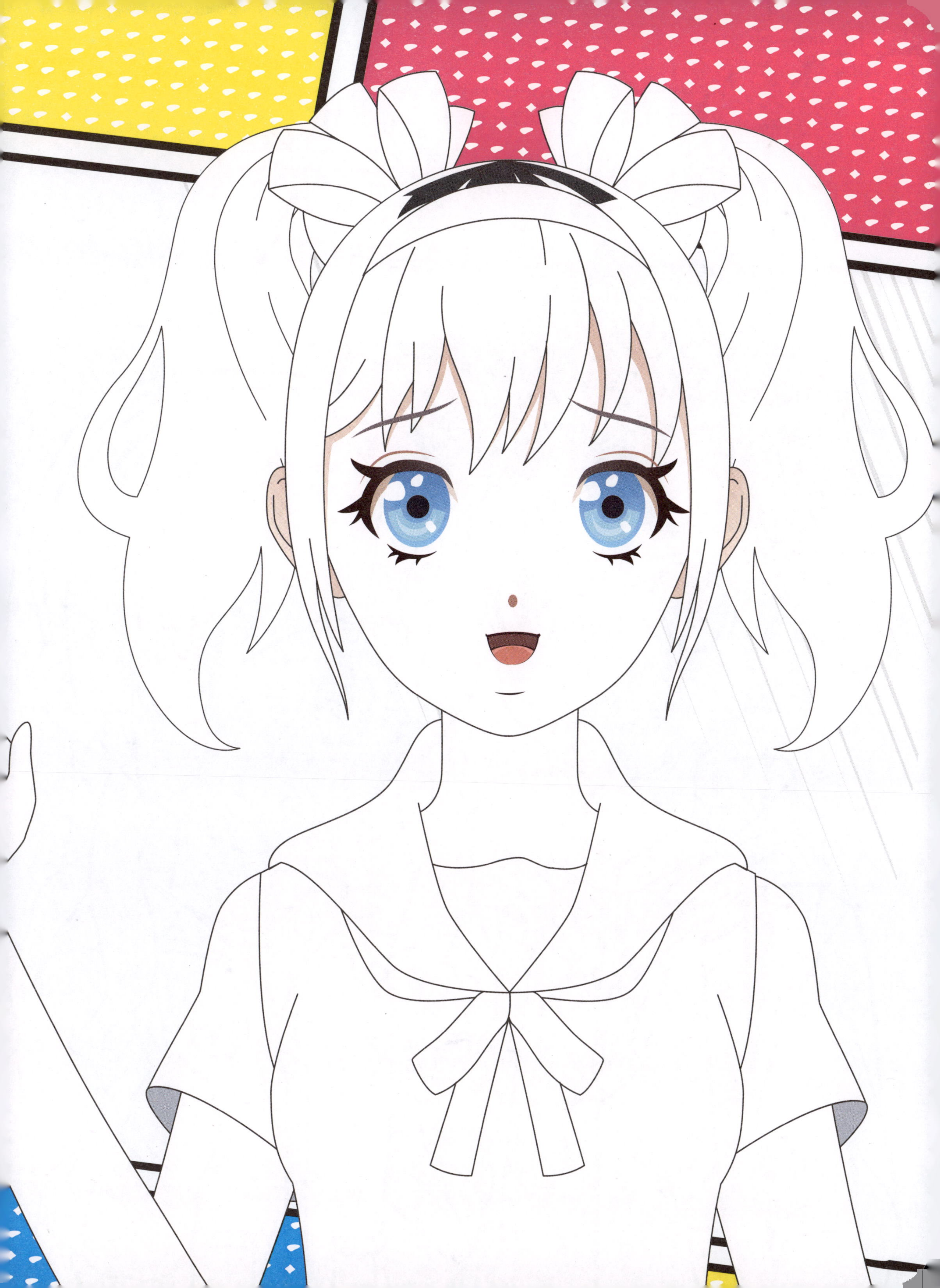

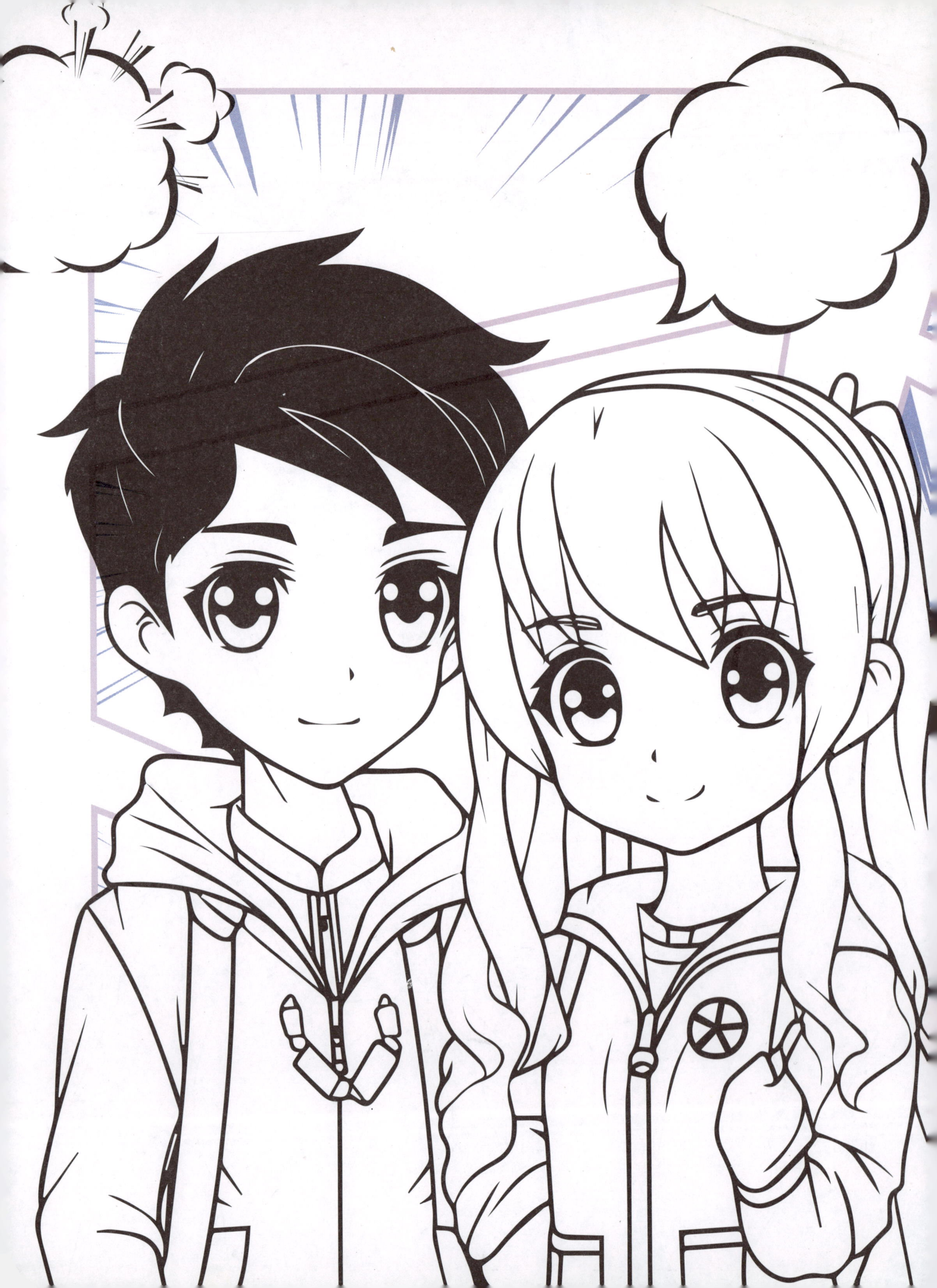